CW01017640

3/23

THRIFTY COOKING

Over 170 reliable recipes and hundreds of budget-friendly hints and tips

MONEY-SAVING

CROWD-PLEASING

LOW-WASTE

COLLECTED WISDOM FROM
THE COUNTRY WOMEN'S ASSOCIATION OF VICTORIA INC.

CONTENTS

The Country Women's Association of Victoria Inc.

A 0004857F   ABN 55 584 949 677

WELCOME TO

The Country Women's Association of Victoria Inc.

The Country Women's Association of Victoria was formed 12 March 1928 and today has approximately 4500 members. We're a vibrant, philanthropic organisation of women supporting women, children and families right across Victoria and we'd love you to join us.

We care, we cook, we craft and we advocate for change, while always remaining relevant.

The Country Women's Association is for all women, all ages and from all places in the country and the city.

Belong to a Branch of the Country Women's Association of Victoria and

- enjoy volunteering to assist those most vulnerable and in need
- create friendships
- learn and share new skills
- be involved in understanding issues impacting on your community and advocate for change

To begin your membership – contact a Branch near you by checking the map on our website or email **membership@cwaofvic.org.au** or ring **03 9827 8971**.

Looking forward to seeing you at your CWA of Victoria event!

Marion Dewar
State President

Pam Mawson
Deputy State President

You become a member of the CWA of Victoria by joining a Branch. You are welcome to visit several Branches to find the Branch that most suits you – every Branch is unique!

https://cwaofvic.org.au/about/become-a-member/

Visit our website to find out more **cwaofvic.org.au**

Visit our Facebook page to see our latest news
https://www.facebook.com/cwaofvic/

WASTE NOT
WANT NOT

VEGETABLES

- Any **vegetables past their best** in the vegie crisper can be made into tasty soup.

- Left-over cooked vegetables can be mashed all together. Heat some oil in a pan and fry like a big pancake. Turn carefully after 5 minutes and fry until crispy and heated through – traditionally called **Bubble and Squeak**. Serve with cooked rashers of bacon (optional).

- Any left-over cooked vegetables can be blended together and added to **stock for a vegetable soup**.

- Use left-over roast veg to make a **roast vegetable salad** or **frittata**.

- For **Roast Vegetable Salad** mix chopped left-over roast vegetables such as potato, pumpkin, carrots, beetroot, parsnips and zucchini (courgettes) with feta cheese and currants and drizzle with a balsamic vinegar dressing.

Roast Vegetable Frittata

- **chopped left-over roast vegetables**
- **butter or oil, for greasing**
- **6 eggs**
- **½ cup (125 ml) pouring cream**
- **finely chopped herbs, such as parsley and basil (optional)**
- **crumbled feta cheese, to taste (optional)**

Spread chopped left-over roast vegetables over the bottom of a greased shallow ovenproof dish.

Beat the eggs and cream and season well with salt and pepper. Pour this mixture over the roast vegetables and bake in a moderate (180°C) oven 20 minutes until set.

Finely chopped fresh herbs such as parsley and basil give extra flavour as does the inclusion of a little feta with the chopped roast vegetables.

- Left-over **vegetable tops** (such as carrot tops) are good bases for stocks and soup.

- Mash and add left-over cooked **pumpkin** to a casserole or soup to help thicken and to add extra flavour.

- If **mushrooms** are starting to shrivel, slice, then cook gently with pouring cream to make a mushroom sauce. Season well with salt and ground white pepper.

- Mushrooms that have shrivelled a little can be added when making a **stock** for extra flavour.

- If you have excess **sweetcorn cobs**, or they are on special to buy, cut the kernels off the corn cob and freeze in ziplock bags until you want to use them. No need to pre-cook. Make sure bag is airtight, vacuum sealed if possible.

- **Vegetable Fritters**
  You can use corn kernels to make vegetable fritters. Whisk 125 ml milk and 125 ml pouring cream, 2 eggs and 150 g plain flour together to make a batter. Season well with salt and pepper. (For a lighter batter, use 1 cup/250 ml soda water instead of the milk and cream.)

- Combine any or all of the following ingredients – sweetcorn kernels (fresh or canned), grated carrot (frozen or fresh), grated zucchini (courgette), feta cheese, finely chopped herbs such as parsley or chives. Fry spoonfuls of the ingredients in hot oil until golden and crispy.

- **Washed potato skins** can be air-fried, or deep-fried in oil, or baked in the oven with oil sprinkled on them before baking as oven-fry chips.

- **Left-over roast or steamed potatoes**
  Melt butter and olive oil together (the oil stops the butter burning but the butter crisps up the potatoes) and, when hot, add chopped cooked potatoes and cook and turn regularly until edges are crispy and potatoes are heated through. For extra flavour sprinkle with Vegeta vegetable seasoning or celery salt. Dried garlic granules are another tasty flavouring.

Potato Bake

- left-over roast potatoes
- butter or oil, for greasing
- peeled and crushed garlic cloves
- salt and pepper to taste
- 300 ml chicken stock
- 300 ml milk
- 2 tablespoons chopped chives
- mustard, such as Dijon
- grated tasty cheese

Slice the potatoes and layer them in a greased casserole dish. Sprinkle each layer with peeled and crushed garlic cloves and salt and pepper to taste.

Mix together the chicken stock and milk, chives and mustard and pour this mixture over the potatoes.

Cover dish with a lid or foil and bake for ¾–1 hour. Uncover the dish and sprinkle with grated tasty cheese. Return to the oven for a further 10 minutes.

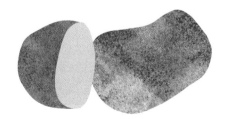

Potato Puffs

A great use for left-over mashed potato (or mashed pumpkin, sweet potato, carrot and parsnip, or any combination of these).

- **45 g butter**
- **½ cup (125 ml) water**
- **self-raising flour (1 tablespoon for every cup/230 g mashed potato)**
- **salt and pepper to taste**
- **1 egg**
- **left-over mashed potato**
- **oil, for frying**

Put the butter and water in a saucepan over a medium heat and bring to the boil. Whisk in the self-raising flour and a good pinch of salt. Whisk until the mixture comes together to form a ball. Remove from the heat.

Cool the mixture, then beat in the egg and left-over mashed potato. Season well with salt and pepper to taste.

Drop spoonfuls of the puff mixture into hot oil and cook until golden. Drain on paper before serving hot.

- Save the **leaves of celery** and chop and put into soup for extra flavouring. The leaves can also be dried and used as a flavouring in soups and casseroles. Place the leaves on an oven tray in a very slow oven (100–110°C) to dry slowly. When dry and cool, store in an airtight container.

- To help stop **celery and carrots** going soft, wrap them in paper towel, then place into an airtight container in the fridge.

- If a **lettuce** becomes limp, refresh it in cold water to which lemon juice has been added.

- Don't waste **broccoli stems**. Peel and slice thinly to add to the vegetables in a stir-fry, or add chopped peeled stems to a vegetable soup or stock.

- If roasting or pickling **beetroot**, don't throw out the tops – use them as a vegetable in a stir-fry or as you would use spinach or silverbeet in a quiche or tart.

- If you grow **leeks** in the garden, and they start to go to seed, dig them up, cut out the core that is going to seed and finely slice the remaining part of the leek. Store in ziplock bags in the freezer for later use in recipes, but double-bag them so that the leek smell doesn't go through the freezer.

- **Berries** past their best can be whizzed in the food processor with icing sugar to taste to make a berry dessert sauce.

- If you warm a slighty shrivelled whole **lemon** for a few seconds in the microwave, or roll it vigorously on the bench before juicing, you get more juice.

- **Citrus peel** can be dried and blended to a powder to add flavour to muesli, or biscuits or cakes.

Candied Peel

Left-over orange peel is good to make candied peel. This is very nice dipped in melted chocolate to serve with coffee after dinner.

- orange peel from 1 orange

- 2 cups (440 g) sugar to 1 cup (250 ml) water

Place the orange peel in a saucepan and cover with water and bring to the boil. Pour off the water and repeat this process to remove any bitterness.

Simmer in fresh water until the peel is tender to the bite. Drain peel. Return the peel to the saucepan with the sugar and water. Starting over a low heat, stir until the sugar has dissolved, then simmer until the peel is translucent. This takes a while. Drain the water off.

Spread the peel onto a wire rack to dry, turning as needed. Store the dry peel in an airtight container.

- **Stew fruit** without sugar and then freeze. Add sugar when you thaw out and want to use the fruit. Fruit that is stewed and frozen without sugar will retain its natural colour. It doesn't darken or 'go pink'. Thaw and use for fruit puddings or crumbles.

- Chop up **banana skins** and use as a fertiliser around plants in the garden. Bananas contain potassium, which promotes fruiting and flowering.

- Use up **overripe bananas** in ice cream – freeze bananas in their skin, then take off the skin and whizz the bananas in a food processor while frozen and they will turn into creamy banana ice cream.

- **Overripe bananas** give better flavour in cooking than underripe ones do.

Broadlands Station Banana Sheet Cake

This cake is mixed all together in a saucepan.

- 125 g butter
- ¾ cup (165 g) caster sugar
- 1 teaspoon pure vanilla essence
- 1 egg
- 2 mashed overripe bananas
- 1½ cups (225 g) self-raising flour
- ¼ cup (60 ml) milk
- lemon icing

In a saucepan melt butter and caster sugar. Add vanilla essence. Beat in egg and bananas, stir in self-raising flour and milk. Mix all together well until smooth.

Bake in a lined 24 cm square slice tin at 170°C for approximately 20–25 minutes. Ice with lemon icing.

• Banana Upside Down Cake

If you have a lot of overripe bananas in the fruit bowl, make a banana upside down cake. Melt a little butter and pour into the lined cake tin you are making your banana cake in. Sprinkle with brown sugar and place slices of banana over the butter and sugar mixture before pouring in your banana cake or loaf mixture. When cooked, tip out onto a plate with the caramel and banana on the top. Serve warm for dessert with cream.

IDEAS FOR USING UP MARMALADE

• If you only have a small amount left in a jar of marmalade and it has hardened, add it to a fruit cake mixture. This will replace a little of the liquid and adds an extra depth of flavour to the fruit cake.

• Left-over marmalade can also replace mixed peel in a fruit cake recipe if you have run out of mixed peel.

• Left-over marmalade can be used to put into the bottom of a pudding steamer before adding the pudding mixture. It makes a nice change from jam. Make a sauce to go with the pudding by heating more marmalade with a little water to make a pouring consistency.

- Excess **chillies can be dried** in a slow (150–160°C) oven, then blended to a powder and stored in an airtight jar. Add a sprinkling for extra heat in a dish.

- **Dry excess herbs** over summer by hanging tied-up bunches upside down in an airy place to dry and then store in a cool dry container for winter use – e.g. parsley and thyme.

- The soft, fleshy, delicate leaves of **basil** can be frozen in ice cubes to be used in winter.

TIP

Wash **parsley** in hot water before chopping. It improves the flavour and makes chopping the parsley easier.

- Always store **pine nuts, walnuts and pecans** in the freezer to stop the oils in them going rancid.

- Grind whole **almonds** in a high-speed blender to make your own almond meal.

- If using **almonds in a fruit cake** it is not necessary to skin them before chopping and adding to the cake mixture. Almonds in skins are cheaper to buy.

RED MEAT

- **Left-over casserole/stew, tagine or curry** can be made into pies. If using a commercial pie maker, use shortcrust pastry on the bottom and puff pastry on the top. Make sure filling is cold before putting it in the pastry in pie maker.

- **Meat paste sandwich filling**
  Left-over roast lamb or beef, or left-over cooked corned beef, can be whizzed up in the food processor with tomato chutney or relish or green tomato pickles – whatever pickles or relish you have open. Whizz in food processor until a good spreading consistency.

- **Slices of left-over roast meat** can be dipped in batter and then lightly fried in hot oil until batter is golden brown.

- Save the **juices from a roast**. Chill in a container in the fridge, take off the fat and discard, then freeze the jellied juices underneath. Makes a delicious stock.

- Any **left-over roast meat or corned silverside** can be sliced and reheated, wrapped in foil, in the oven for another meal.

- If you have **left-over corned silverside**, slice and wrap in foil with any left-over cheese or mustard sauce to heat in the oven. Likewise roast lamb or beef can be reheated in the oven, with some left-over gravy, wrapped in foil.

Spicy Moroccan Lamb One Pot

Instead of using fresh lamb, cook vegetables and make as per recipe, but add chopped left-over cooked roast lamb and heat through.

SERVES 4

- 1 tablespoon olive oil
- 500 g diced lamb, tossed in seasoned flour
- 2 diced carrots
- 1 green capsicum (pepper), deseeded and cut into strips
- 1 chopped onion
- 2 garlic cloves, crushed
- 3 cups (750 ml) chicken stock
- 1 tablespoon Moroccan seasoning (chermoula)
- 400 g can of chickpeas
- ¾ cup (140 g) couscous
- 1 cup (30 g) chopped flat-leaf parsley
- ¼ cup (30 g) slivered almonds

Heat oil in a casserole dish and add lamb. Cook until browned, then remove and set aside. Add vegetables and garlic to casserole and cook until softened. Stir in stock and seasoning and bring to the boil. Lower to a simmer and return the lamb to the pot. Cover and cook for 1 hour or until lamb is tender.

Stir in chickpeas and couscous, cover and cook for 5 minutes. Season and add three-quarters of the parsley and stir through. Cook in 175°C oven or in a slow cooker. Serve with remainder of parsley and almonds sprinkled on top.

Lamb Curry

You can use left-over roast lamb here. Make sauce and cook and
add chopped left-over roast lamb and heat through.

SERVES 4

- 5 tablespoons canola oil
- 500 g boneless lamb, cut into cubes
- 1 tablespoon mustard seeds
- ½ tablespoon fenugreek seeds
- curry leaves
- 3 green chillies, deseeded and sliced
- 2 tablespoons finely chopped ginger
- ½ tablespoon turmeric powder
- 1 tablespoon curry powder
- 1 tablespoon freshly ground black pepper
- 3 onions, roughly chopped
- 1 tin (400 g) whole peeled tomatoes
- 1 tin (400 ml) coconut milk
- salt
- coriander leaves, for garnish

Heat oil in a large saucepan, add lamb cubes and fry until slightly golden. Add mustard seeds, fenugreek seeds and stir-fry for another 2–3 minutes. Add curry leaves, green chilli, ginger, turmeric, curry powder and pepper and stir well.

In a food processor, chop the onions further and add the tin of tomatoes and process until onions are quite fine. Add this mixture to the lamb, add the coconut milk and add salt to taste. Stir well and cook over a low heat or in a slow (150–160°C) oven until the meat is tender.

When cooked serve with steamed rice and top with the chopped coriander leaves for decoration.

Shepherd's Pie

Left-over roast lamb or beef can be minced in the food processor to make a shepherd's pie.

- 1 finely diced carrot
- 2 sticks finely chopped celery
- 1 peeled and finely chopped brown onion
- olive oil
- 2 peeled and crushed garlic cloves
- 1 chicken stock cube or 1 teaspoon stock powder
- left-over roast meat, minced
- Gravox (gravy powder) and cornflour for thickening
- mashed potato
- butter
- tasty cheese, grated

Sauté the carrot, celery and onion in a little olive oil until soft. Add the garlic and stock cube or stock powder. Add minced roast meat and 1 cup (250 ml) water. Cook until vegetables are soft.

Thicken the juices with a little Gravox and cornflour mixed to a paste in a little cold water.

Pour mixture into a greased ovenproof dish. Cover with mashed potato. Dot a little butter on the mashed potato, cover with grated tasty cheese and heat in a moderate (180°C) oven about 20 minutes to melt the cheese and heat through.

Note: Left-over tomato passata may be used instead of water. Left-over cooked carrots, parsnips, turnips or swede can be mashed in with the potato to add extra flavour.

Spiced-up Cottage Pie with Surprise Mash

SERVES 6

- 3 tablespoons oil
- 600 g lamb mince
- 1 large onion, finely diced
- 2 garlic cloves, finely chopped
- 1 tablespoon fresh ginger, finely grated
- 2 tablespoons ground cumin
- ½ tablespoon ground cinnamon
- 2 tablespoons tomato paste
- 1 large carrot, grated
- 400 g can crushed tomatoes
- 3 cups (750 ml) vegetable stock
- 1 tablespoon chopped rosemary
- ½ cup (30 g) chopped parsley
- cooked carrots and parsnip, or cooked sweet potato, for mashing
- butter
- milk

Heat half the oil in a large frying pan over a high heat. Season the lamb with salt and pepper and fry in two batches until well browned. Set aside.

Drain off any fat from the pan, add the remaining oil and cook the onion. When the onion is soft, add garlic, ginger, cumin and cinnamon and cook over a low heat for another couple of minutes. Add the tomato paste and stir over the heat for 2 minutes. Add the browned lamb, carrot, tomatoes, stock and rosemary and simmer for about 30 minutes, stirring regularly until a thick meaty sauce. Mix in the parsley and check seasoning and adjust to taste.

Place this mixture in a baking dish and top with cooked carrots and parsnips mashed together with lots of butter and a little milk OR mashed sweet potato. Bake in a moderate (180°C) oven until piping hot and top is nicely browned (approximately 40 minutes).

· If you have **left-over savoury mince or bolognese sauce** or left-over Middle Eastern flavoured lamb mince:

① Turn into pastry turnovers by cutting one or more sheets of thawed-out frozen puff pastry into 4 squares. Place a small amount of the left-over mixture on the square, fold over, brush with an egg wash made from 1 egg beaten with a little milk, and bake in a moderate (180°C) oven for approximately 15 minutes.

② Make toasted jaffles.

③ Put mince into an ovenproof dish and spread mashed potato on top, sprinkle on tasty cheese and bake to heat through as a shepherd's pie.

④ Toast a split English muffin. Put on hot left-over savoury mince or bolognese sauce, add a pineapple ring on top, some sliced ham and top with grated cheese and melt the cheese under a grill before serving.

⑤ Bake potatoes in the oven. When cooked, split and cover the cooked potato halves with some left-over savoury mince or bolognese sauce.

⑥ Cut a red capsicum (pepper) in half lengthways, take out the seeds and membrane, fill with left-over savoury mince or bolognese sauce, sprinkle with grated cheese and finely chopped parsley and bake in a moderate (180°C) oven for approximately 25 minutes until cheese is melted and mixture is piping hot and capsicum soft.

Lunchtime 'Pizza Pie'

- 125 g butter
- 5 tablespoons milk
- 1½ cups (225 g) self-raising flour
- left-over bolognese sauce
- 420 g tin sweetcorn, drained (optional)
- grated tasty cheese, for topping

Heat butter and milk, and as soon as the butter has melted remove from the stove and add the flour. Mix until smooth. Press into a greased lamington tin 30 cm x 20 cm. Spread the left-over bolognese sauce over the top.

Spread over the sweetcorn (optional). Sprinkle with tasty cheese and bake in a moderate (180°C) oven for approximately 30 minutes.

- If you have **left-over cooked chicken pieces**, wrap in foil with some sweet chilli sauce and ginger. Heat in the oven to serve.

TIP

To **liven up roast chicken** mash ½ ripe avocado with 2 teaspoons curry powder, add ½ cup (125 g) mayonnaise and mix well. Spread over the fresh chicken then roast as normal.

- **Chicken wings** – keep the tips to go into a soup or to make stock.

- If only a little chicken is left on a cooked chicken, pull it off and chop finely. Mix in a little mayonnaise and a little mango or peach chutney to moisten, and season with salt and pepper to make a **tasty sandwich filling**. Then use the chicken carcase to make chicken stock.

- After deboning a chicken or chicken pieces for a recipe, **use the bones as a stock base**. Use the cooked chicken bones and the little meat left on them to make a tasty stock and freeze.

Chicken Stock

- chicken wing tips, cooked chicken carcases or pieces
- water
- 2 carrots, roughly chopped
- 1 stick celery, roughly chopped, including leaves
- 2 onions, roughly chopped
- carrot tops, parsley stalks, wilted vegies in the crisper – including mushrooms, parsnips, broccoli, zucchini (courgette), pumpkin, swede, turnips
- salt and ground white pepper

Put chicken wing tips, cooked carcases or pieces that you have saved up in the freezer, into a large pot. Three-quarters fill with water, bring to the boil and add carrots, celery including the leaves, onions, and any or all of carrot tops, parsley stalks, left-over wilted vegies. Use whatever you have on hand.

Bring to the boil, and simmer gently for 3 hours. Season well with lots of salt and ground white pepper.

Strain off the chicken and vegies, cool and then chill in the fridge.

Skim off any fat that settles on the top and either use straight away or freeze in 2 cup (500 ml) containers for convenient use in recipes.

Note: You can serve the chicken stock as a broth, and add left-over small pasta shapes to make it more substantial.

Chicken Soup

- 8 cups (2 litres) chicken stock, strained
- 1 finely diced and peeled onion
- 1 peeled and finely diced carrot
- 2 finely diced sticks of celery
- 2 finely diced chicken breasts or left-over cooked chicken
- 1 or 2 packets chicken noodle soup or Dutch curry and rice soup (optional)
- red lentils – add 1 cup (205 g) for a thicker soup (optional)

To the stock, add the onion, carrot, celery and chicken. Cook until vegetables are soft.

For extra flavour you can add 1 or 2 packets chicken noodle soup or 1 or 2 packets Dutch curry and rice soup. (Left-over cooked small pasta such as macaroni is also a good addition.)

You can add red lentils at the time of adding the vegetables if you would like a thicker soup. They take about 30 minutes to cook.

- If you have cooked too much **bacon and eggs** at breakfast, you can turn them into toasted sandwiches for lunch. Or, cut the crusts off thin sliced bread, roll the bread slices flat with a rolling pin, cut slits in the corners on the diagonal to fit into greased American muffin tins, spread the base with bar-b-q sauce, add the left-over bacon and eggs. Sprinkle with chopped parsley and grated cheese and heat in a moderate (180°C) oven until the cheese has melted and bread has crisped up (about 20 minutes).

TIP

To check the freshness of an egg place the egg in a bowl of cold water. If the egg floats to the top it will be off. Throw it out (carefully!).

- If you have whisked an egg to brush pastry with before baking and have **egg mixture left over**, don't throw it out but turn into a scrambled egg for lunch or breakfast.

- **Left-over egg whites** can be used to make pavlova OR meringues OR lemon mousse.

- **Left-over egg yolks** can be used in place of some of the whole eggs in a recipe for quiche or egg and bacon pie.

- **Egg yolks** can be used to brush over a pastry case to seal it, OR use as an egg wash to brush over a pie to give a nice shine and help the pastry brown.

Chocolate Mousse

If you have egg yolks left over, don't throw them out, make a chocolate mousse.

- **185 g dark or milk chocolate**
- **4 eggs yolks**
- **½ cup (125 ml) water**
- **300 ml pouring cream**
- **½ cup (115 g) caster sugar**
- **½ teaspoon cinnamon**

Melt the chocolate over a pan of hot water, cool slightly. Beat in egg yolks and water and cook over the pan of hot water until this chocolate custard thickens. Chill. Whip the cream with the caster sugar and cinnamon. Gently fold into the chocolate custard mixture and chill.

This can be spread over a pavlova and decorated with fruit, or crush meringues and layer meringue, mousse and berries into glass dessert bowls.

· Freeze eggs

If the chooks are laying well and you can't use all the eggs produced, freeze them. Break very fresh eggs into patty pans sitting in a patty pan tin, then place tin in freezer. When eggs are frozen, remove from the patty papers and store in an airtight container in the freezer. To use, thaw the frozen eggs in a bowl and use as you would fresh ones.

- If **cream is past the use-by date** and has 'soured' a little it can be used to make scones or can be used to make sour cream pastry (below), as long as it hasn't gone mouldy.

Sour Cream Pastry

- ¾ cup (110 g) plain flour
- ¾ cup (110 g) self-raising flour
- 3 tablespoons butter, melted
- ¾ cup (185 g) sour cream

Mix all ingredients together. Rest the pastry at least 10 minutes before using. Roll out pastry between 2 pieces of baking paper.

This is a very good all purpose pastry for both sweet and savoury recipes. Resting the pastry relaxes the gluten in the flour. If you use pastry immediately after making, it will shrink as the gluten hasn't had time to relax.

- **If you don't have any sour cream** for a recipe, plain yoghurt can be substituted.

- **You can 'sour' cream** by measuring required amount of cream and adding either a squeeze of lemon juice or a little white vinegar and let it sit for a few minutes.

- If a recipe calls for buttermilk, you can **'sour' milk** the same way as the sour cream (see opposite) to use in place of buttermilk. The soured milk will then make for a lighter pancake batter or scone mixture.

- If you have **too much milk**, make pancakes.

Basic Pancake Mix

- 1 cup (150 g) plain flour
- ¼ teaspoon salt
- 1 egg
- 250–300 ml milk

Mix all together to form a smooth thin batter. Drop spoonfuls of the mixture into a non-stick or lightly buttered pan and cook.

To make pikelets – use a little less milk to make a stiffer batter and add 1 dessertspoon caster sugar. Cook as for pancakes.

• If you have **excess milk and cream**, make a creamy custard.

Creamy Custard

MAKES 4 CUPS (1 LITRE)

- 2 cups (500 ml) milk, plus a little extra
- 2 cups (500 ml) pouring cream
- 2 eggs, beaten
- 2 tablespoons caster sugar
- 2 tablespoons custard powder

Heat the milk and cream in a saucepan.

In a bowl, beat the eggs and sugar, add the custard powder and mix to a smooth paste with a little more milk.

Pour some of the hot milk into the egg mix and beat. Don't add egg mixture to hot milk as egg will curdle. Always pour some hot milk into the egg mix first. If the mixture does curdle, just beat it really well.

Pour mixture back into the saucepan and cook, stirring constantly, until thickened.

TIP

When making an egg custard, pour some of the hot milk onto the beaten eggs and sugar, beating as you pour, then pour this back into the saucepan and cook very gently, stirring constantly until it thickens. If you pour the cold eggs and sugar mixture into the hot milk, the custard will curdle. OR you can mix the full custard mixture together well before starting to heat, then keep stirring constantly until the custard has cooked and thickened.

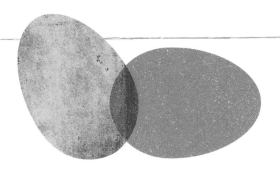

- Use **dried-up cheese or cheese rind** in stocks, casseroles, or boil in the water with pasta to give extra flavour.

- If you have **excess cheese**, make a cheese sauce.

Cheese Sauce

- 2 tablespoons butter
- 2 tablespoons plain flour
- 2 cups (500 ml) milk, plus extra if needed
- 1 cup (125 g) grated tasty cheese
- ½ teaspoon Dijon mustard
- ground white pepper

Melt the butter in a saucepan. Add the flour and stir to mix in and 'cook' the flour for a minute. Gradually add the milk and beat with a whisk until smooth. Add cheese, mustard and white pepper to taste. If too thick add more milk until desired consistency is reached, whisking to make the sauce smooth.

- If you have **cooked too much rice**, use the leftovers to make a salad, stuffed tomatoes, zucchini (courgette) or capsicums (peppers), or a rice custard.

- **Left-over cooked rice or cooked pasta** can be added to a basic custard mixture.

Simple Egg Custard

- 4 cups (1 litre) milk
- 3 tablespoons cornflour
- 4 eggs
- 80 g caster sugar
- pure vanilla essence to taste

Heat almost all the milk in the top of a double saucepan.

Blend cornflour with the remaining cold milk. Blend in a little of the hot milk. Return to saucepan and stir, cook for about 1 minute.

Add egg and sugar beaten together. Cook until custard coats the back of the spoon. Stir in vanilla essence.

• Left-over cooked pasta or rice can be added to **meatballs** to make them go further.

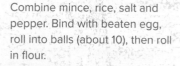

Porcupine Meatballs

- **500 g lean mince steak**
- **¾ cup (165 g) short-grain white rice (or left-over cooked rice)**
- **salt and pepper to taste**
- **1 egg, beaten**
- **¼ cup (35 g) self-raising flour**
- **425 g tin tomato soup**

Combine mince, rice, salt and pepper. Bind with beaten egg, roll into balls (about 10), then roll in flour.

Prepare soup as per instructions on the label. When nearly boiling, place the prepared meatballs into soup and simmer for about 20–25 minutes.

The meatballs can be placed in a casserole dish and cooked in a slow (150–160°C) oven for about 30–40 minutes.

Tuna and Rice Salad

- **1 onion, chopped**
- **15 g butter**
- **1½ cups (280 g) left-over cooked brown rice**
- **220 g can tuna, drained**
- **4 silverbeet leaves, cooked**
- **¼ cup (30 g) grated cheese**
- **¼ cup (60 ml) French dressing**

Cook onion in butter until golden brown. Combine brown rice, tuna and silverbeet in a bowl with grated cheese and French dressing. Add cooked onion and toss well.

- **Stuffed Capsicums**
  Cut top off capsicums (peppers), remove seeds and blanch in hot water for 1 minute. Drain and fill with mixture of cooked rice, onion, mushrooms, parsley, thyme and cumin. Place stuffed capsicums in an ovenproof dish and partially cover with a can of tomato soup. Bake in 200°C oven 30 minutes.

- **Freeze left-over cooked rice or cooked pasta** in ziplock bags. The cooked rice or pasta can then form the base for a quickly prepared meal. Add pesto of any flavour to hot left-over cooked pasta, mix through and sprinkle with grated parmesan cheese for an easy meal. Left-over cooked rice can be made into fried rice.

Fried Rice

Sauté the red onion, celery and capsicum in a little grapeseed oil (not olive oil as it has too strong a flavour for this dish) until soft, add bacon and cook. Add the rice with the remaining ingredients, except soy sauce. Mix gently until heated through, then add 1 tablespoon (or more to taste) light soy sauce.

Note: A little sesame oil added when sautéing the vegetables also adds a little more flavour.

- **1 red onion, finely diced**
- **½ cup (70 g) chopped celery**
- **1 red or green capsicum (pepper), chopped and deseeded**
- **grapeseed oil**
- **2 rashers bacon, rind removed and diced**
- **left-over cooked rice**
- **½ cup (100 g) tinned or freshly cooked corn**
- **½ cup (80 g) frozen peas**
- **1 spring onion, sliced**
- **1 tablespoon light soy sauce, plus extra if needed**

• **If you have cooked too much pasta** – use up in a summer pasta salad (see below) or tuna noodle casserole (see page 44; substitute cooked pasta for the noodles).

Summer Pasta

- 3 cups (465 g) macaroni pasta, cooked
  (1½ cups uncooked)
- 2 cups (180 g) button mushrooms, sliced
- 1 red capsicum (pepper), chopped
- 125 g salami or ham, cut into thin strips
- 3 spring onions, chopped
- ⅓ cup (80 ml) cream-style dressing

Combine all salad ingredients and dressing.
Chill if required and serve.

TIP

A great way to utilise **left-over pasta** is to add a few fresh ingredients and dressing.

Tuna Noodle Casserole

- ⅓ cup (80 ml) oil
- 250 g fine egg noodles
- 500 g canned tuna, drained
- 310 g canned cream of celery soup
- 3 sticks celery, thinly sliced (optional)
- 60 g salted cashews
- ¼ cup (60 ml) lemon juice
- pepper
- water as needed

Heat the oil in a frying pan, add the noodles and fry gently until just starting to brown, turning the noodles as they are browning. Remove frying pan from the heat.

Add the drained tuna, soup, celery, cashews, lemon juice and pepper. Return the pan to the heat and simmer for 15 minutes, adding water only if needed.

- **Fruit bread, raisin toast or hot cross buns** that have gone stale make a delicious bread and butter pudding.

- **Bread and Butter Pudding**
  Butter bread, then spread with a little of any jam you have open in the cupboard. Cut bread slices into small pieces and arrange in a greased ovenproof dish. Make a custard with 1 egg for every cup (250 ml) of milk and a little sugar. Beat eggs, sugar and milk and carefully pour over bread. Bake in a moderate (180°C) oven for approximately 30 minutes until custard has set. For a dish 15 cm x 18 cm x 6 cm deep use 2 slices bread or fruit bread, 2 eggs and 2 cups (500 ml) milk. This will give a generous serve for 3 people. Multiply the amount and the size of the dish used to be enough for the number of people you are serving.

- **If using plain stale bread for a bread and butter pudding**, sprinkle on some sultanas after you have placed the cut up bread and butter in the dish. Jam is optional. Make a custard and pour over bread and bake.

- **To refresh stale bread** sprinkle with a little water and heat in a moderate (180°C) oven for about 10 minutes.

- **Use stale bread to make croutons**
  Cut stale bread into 2 cm dice. Mix with chopped dried thyme, rosemary or oregano. Sprinkle with olive oil and then place on a greased oven tray. Bake in a moderate (180°C) oven until golden brown. Drain on absorbent paper, then store in an airtight container when cool.

- **Stale bread** can be used to make breadcrumbs, fresh or dried.

- **Don't throw out bread crusts**. Whizz in food processor to make fresh breadcrumbs or dry in a low (150–160°C) oven until crispy then whizz in food processor to make dry breadcrumbs and store in an airtight container.

Curried Breadcrumbs

- ⅓ cup (90 g) butter
- 2 teaspoons curry powder
- 2 cups (160 g) fresh breadcrumbs
- oil for frying

Melt butter, add curry powder, then add breadcrumbs and mix. Gently fry this mixture in a little oil until crisp. Use as a topping on a salad instead of croutons, on the top of savoury tarts or on the top of casseroles.

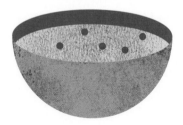

- **Stale bread** can be toasted, torn into pieces and used in a tomato bread salad.

Tomato Bread Salad

- torn toasted bread
- 3 large tomatoes
- ½ cup (125 ml) water
- ½ capsicum (pepper), deseeded and chopped
- 1 red onion, chopped
- 1 clove garlic, crushed
- 1 tablespoon capers, chopped
- 3 drained chopped anchovies
- 1 small cucumber, chopped
- ⅓ cup (80 ml) olive oil
- 1 tablespoon red wine vinegar

Place bread in a bowl. Puree one of the tomatoes with the water and pour over the bread. Combine capsicum, onion, garlic, capers, anchovies, cucumber, oil and vinegar and add to the bowl with the bread.

Remove the seeds from the remaining tomatoes and chop them. Stir the chopped tomatoes into all the other ingredients.

· **Broken biscuits** can be used to make a base for a cheesecake or a slice.

Fruit Salad Slice

- 1 packet Sao biscuits or the equivalent in broken biscuits
- 1 tin fruit salad
- 3 tablespoons custard powder
- a little cold water to mix the custard powder
- whipped cream, to serve

Spread the biscuits out in a slice container (if using Sao biscuits you may need to cut them to fit the container).

Put the fruit salad, juice and all, in a small saucepan.

Blend the custard powder with the water and stir into the fruit salad on a medium heat, stirring until it boils and thickens.

Spread over the biscuits and refrigerate to cool. When cold either cover with whipped cream or put a 'dollop' of whipped cream on when serving.

- Don't waste **pastry scraps**. Re-roll and, if only a little left, spread half with jam, sprinkle grated apple on top, fold over and bake as a turnover.

- If **not enough pastry** to roll out to a full cover on a pie, cut into strips and make a lattice pattern over the pie and bake as normal.

- If left-over pastry is puff pastry, re-roll and cut into rectangles and bake to make **matchsticks**. When cooked pastry is cold, split and spread with jam and whipped cream. Put on the lid and dust with a little icing sugar.

LIGHT MEALS:
SOUPS, SNACKS AND SMOKO

Spicy Red Lentil Soup

SERVES 4–6

- 1 tablespoon vegetable oil
- 1 brown onion, peeled and finely chopped
- 1 clove garlic, peeled and crushed
- ¼ cup (60 g) red korma curry paste
- 1 litre vegetable stock
- 400 g can diced tomatoes
- ⅔ cup (145 g) red lentils, rinsed
- ¼ cup (55 g) pearl barley, rinsed
- 1 each carrot, leek and celery stick, all finely diced
- yoghurt and chopped coriander to serve (optional)

Heat oil, cook the onion and garlic until softened. Add curry paste, stir to combine. Stir in stock, tomatoes, lentils, barley and vegetables. Bring to the boil then reduce heat to a simmer for about 20–30 minutes.

Serve with a dollop of yoghurt and chopped coriander (optional).

Eileen's Canadian Corn Chowder

SERVES 4

- 2 slices bacon
- oil, for frying
- ½ cup (80 g) chopped onion
- ¾ cup (90 g) sliced celery
- 1 cup (140 g) peeled and diced potatoes
- pinch cayenne pepper
- pinch pepper
- 1 teaspoon salt (or to taste)
- 2–3 tablespoons plain flour
- 2 cups (500 ml) milk
- 1 large can corn kernels
- 1 tablespoon finely chopped red capsicum (pepper)
- 1 tablespoon chopped parsley

Cut the bacon into 1 cm strips and fry in oil until crisp. Add onion, celery, potatoes and brown lightly. Add seasonings and ½ cup (125 ml) water. Cover and simmer until vegetables are just cooked.

Blend flour with a little milk. Add remaining milk to the vegetables and stir in the blended flour and milk until the mixture boils. Simmer 3 minutes.

Add drained corn, capsicum and parsley. Serve very hot.

Edwina's Ravioli Soup

SERVES 6-8

- any left-over vegetables or
vegetables past their best in the crisper
- 1 carton (1 litre) beef stock
- 1 tin (400 g) chopped tomatoes
- 1 jar (300 g) medium salsa
- 1 packet (200 g) kids' ravioli

Place all together in a pot and simmer until
vegetables are cooked through. Add a little extra
water if the soup is too thick.

Serve with parsley pesto, garlic or cheese toast
and a sprinkle of parmesan cheese.

Chicken Minestrone

- 1 tablespoon olive oil
- 1 onion, diced
- 1 leek, chopped
- 1 green capsicum (pepper), diced
- 2 cloves garlic, crushed
- 1 large sweet potato
- 2 celery sticks
- 3 large carrots, diced
- 2 cups (150 g) cabbage
- 4 chicken breast fillets
- 3 zucchini (courgettes), diced
- 2½ cups (625 ml) chicken stock
- 420 g can peeled tomatoes
- ¾ cup (115 g) macaroni
- 440 g can cannellini beans
- ½ cup (110 g) short-grain white rice
- parsley, chopped
- parmesan cheese, grated

Heat oil in soup pot, add onion, leek, capsicum and garlic and fry for 2–3 minutes. Cube sweet potato, celery and carrots, shred cabbage and add to pot. Cook for 5 minutes.

Cut chicken into bite-sized pieces and add to pot. Cook to seal on all sides. Cut zucchini into cubes and add to pot. Cook for 5 minutes.

Add the chicken stock and tomatoes. Simmer, covered, for 1–1½ hours. Add macaroni, beans and rice and simmer for a further 15–20 minutes. Serve sprinkled with parsley and parmesan. Can be frozen in portions and reheated when required. Can use diced steak instead of chicken.

Note: When adding macaroni, other pasta, beans and rice, add extra stock if soup is too thick for your taste.

Curried Cauliflower Soup

SERVES 6

- 1 whole cauliflower
- 30 g butter
- 2 teaspoons curry powder
- 4 cups (1 litre) chicken stock
- ½ cup (125 ml) milk
- 2 egg yolks (optional)
- ½ cup (125 ml) pouring cream
- parsley, chopped
- pinch nutmeg
- salt and pepper to taste

Remove outside leaves from cauliflower and break into florets. Reserve a few florets for garnish. Drop cauliflower into a pan of boiling, salted water and cook until tender, about 10 minutes. Drain and press through sieve or blender.

Melt butter and lightly fry curry powder for a few minutes. Add stock and bring slowly to the boil. Add milk and cauliflower. Combine egg yolks (if using) with cream and some of the hot soup. Blend well and return this to the pan. Cook gently, stirring until soup thickens without boiling. Garnish with parsley, season with nutmeg, salt and pepper, then serve immediately.

Curried Carrot and Leek Soup

SERVES 10

- 50 g butter
- 1 tablespoon curry powder
- 2 leeks, washed well and sliced
- 1.5 kg carrots, peeled and sliced
- 1.5 litres chicken stock
- ¼ teaspoon ground cumin
- salt and pepper, to taste
- ¼ cup (30 g) skim milk powder
- 2 cups (500 ml) skim milk
- 300 g light sour cream
- 2 tablespoons chopped parsley and/or chives

Melt butter in a large saucepan and sauté the curry powder, leeks and carrots for 5 minutes. Add the stock and simmer, covered, for 25–30 minutes, until the carrots are tender. Stir in the cumin and seasoning.

Puree this mixture and return to the clean pan.

Mix the powdered milk into the milk and blend, then add to the soup and reheat without boiling.

Combine sour cream and herbs until smooth.

Serve soup garnished with a spoonful of sour cream and herb mixture.

Mini Crustless Quiches

MAKES ABOUT 16

- 4 eggs
- 1 cup (250 ml) skim or whole milk
- ½ cup (125 ml) pouring cream
- 2 tablespoons self-raising flour
- 1 tablespoon chicken stock powder
- finely chopped parsley
- salt and pepper to taste
- 2½ cups (375 g) cooked and cooled left-over vegetables – e.g. corn, onion, peas, pumpkin or sweet potato, spinach or silverbeet
- 3 rashers bacon, chopped and fried OR 1 cup (150 g) left-over cooked chicken, chopped
- 1 cup (125 g) grated tasty cheese
- 16 tomato slices (optional)

Preheat oven to 180°C.

Beat eggs with milk and cream, then gradually add flour, stock powder, parsley and seasoning.

Spray muffin pans with non-stick spray. Mix vegetables and bacon with the cheese.

Fill the muffin pans ⅔ full with the vegetable mixture, carefully pour over the egg mixture. Arrange a tomato slice on top (optional). Cook about 20 minutes or until egg mixture is set.

Vegetarian Pizza Pie

SERVES 4

- 1 large tablespoon oil or butter
- ¾ teacup (70 g) self-raising flour
- ½ teaspoon of salt
- milk or water, to mix to a firm dough

TOPPING
- 1 medium onion, chopped
- 200 g chopped mushrooms
- 1 roasted capsicum (pepper), chopped
- tomato slices
- 125 g grated tasty cheese
- oregano or basil
- salt and pepper

Rub oil or butter into flour, add salt and mix with milk or water. Knead well, roll out and spread on pizza tray.

Spread the onion, mushrooms and capsicum over dough. Next, add the slices of tomato, cheese, oregano or basil, then season. Cook for 30 minutes in a 200°C oven. Cut into squares for suppers or afternoon teas.

Note: Add strips of bacon if not making vegetarian.

Time-poor Sausage Rolls

MAKES 36 SMALL SAUSAGE ROLLS

- 6 sheets frozen puff pastry
- 12 thick lamb sausages
- jar of onion relish or onion jam
- tomato sauce
- beaten egg, for brushing

Thaw the pastry sheets and cut each sheet in half.

Skin the sausages and lay on the pastry sheet. Spread over some of the onion relish or onion jam. Squirt on a little tomato sauce and roll mixture into a sausage roll shape. Cut each roll into thirds.

Brush with beaten egg, place on a greased oven tray and bake in a moderate (180°C) oven for 25 minutes.

Beef and Caramelised Onion Sausage Rolls

MAKES 32 SMALL SAUSAGE ROLLS

- 1 kg beef mince
- 1 tablespoon Worcestershire sauce
- 4 tablespoons caramelised onions or onion relish
- 1 large grated carrot
- 1 grated zucchini (courgette)
- 1 cup (80 g) fresh breadcrumbs
- 2 tablespoons finely chopped parsley
- salt and pepper to taste
- 4 sheets frozen puff pastry, thawed
- 1 egg beaten with a little milk, for brushing
- poppy or sesame seeds, for sprinkling

Mix all ingredients, except pastry, egg and poppy seeds, together well with your hands.

Cut each pastry sheet in half and place a 'sausage' of the mixture along the edge of each half. Roll up. Slice each roll into 4.

Place on a lined baking tray. With a pastry brush, brush each sausage roll with an egg wash of 1 egg beaten with a little milk. Leave plain or sprinkle with either poppy or sesame seeds. Bake in a moderate (180°C) oven 25 minutes or until golden brown and cooked through.

Lamby Muffins

MAKES 12

- 500 g lamb mince
- 1 onion
- 1 grated carrot
- 1 small zucchini (courgette), grated
- oil, for frying
- 1 packet taco seasoning, Moroccan seasoning or mixed herbs
- packet 6 English muffins
- tomato paste
- grated cheese

Fry up the lamb mince, onion and vegies in a little oil until lamb is cooked through and vegies soft. Keep stirring to break up any lumps. Sprinkle in a little taco seasoning – more or less depending on taste – and stir through and cook a few minutes longer.

Cut muffins in half and place on oven trays. Spread each half with some tomato paste, spoon on lamb mixture, sprinkle with grated cheese and heat in moderate (180°C) oven until hot and cheese melted and golden brown.

· Lamby Pizzas

Spread pizza bases with tomato paste and spread on the Lamby Muffin mixture (see opposite), sprinkle with grated tasty cheese and mozzarella cheese and heat in the oven until bubbling hot and cheese has melted (about 20 minutes).

· Lamby Pinwheels

Using the mixture from Lamby Muffins (see opposite), spread sheets of puff pastry with tomato paste. Spread over cooled lamb mince mixture, sprinkle with grated cheese, roll the sheets into a log and cut them into 2 cm wide pieces. Place cut-side up on a greased oven tray and bake in a moderate (180°C) oven until pastry puffed and golden brown.

Cheese and Herb Bread Pudding

SERVES 6

- 680 g sliced loaf of bread
- ½ cup (60 ml) melted butter
- 3 eggs
- 2½ cups (625 ml) milk
- 1 cup (125 g) grated tasty cheese
- ½ cup (125 ml) pouring cream
- 1 tablespoon chopped fresh herbs
- pinch paprika

Remove crusts and cut each slice of bread into four. Arrange bread in a greased 1 litre capacity ovenproof dish. Pour butter carefully over bread.

Mix eggs, milk, cheese, cream and herbs and pour over bread. Sprinkle paprika on top. Bake at 180°C for 45–50 minutes. Serve with garden salad or as an accompaniment to casseroles.

Ham and Asparagus Bake

SERVES 4

- 2 cups (270 g) diced cooked ham
- 2 cups (370 g) cooked short-grain white rice
- ½ cup (60 g) shredded cheese
- ½ cup (125 ml) pouring cream or evaporated milk
- 1 can condensed cream of asparagus soup (undiluted)
- 2 tablespoons grated onion
- ¾ cup (35 g) cornflake crumbs, or crushed potato chips (crisps)
- 3 tablespoons melted butter, plus extra for greasing
- asparagus spears or parsley sprigs, to garnish

Combine ham, rice, cheese, cream, soup and onion. Pour into an ovenproof dish greased with butter.

Mix cornflake crumbs or potato chips with melted butter, and sprinkle over the casserole. Bake in a moderate (180°C) oven until thoroughly heated and top is tinted a pale gold. Garnish with asparagus spears or parsley sprigs.

Corn and Tomato Savoury

SERVES 2

- 1 tin sweetcorn kernels
- 2 eggs, beaten
- 1 or 2 rashers bacon, chopped and cooked
- 1 teaspoon grated onion
- salt and pepper to taste
- 3 medium tomatoes, peeled and sliced
- ½ cup (40 g) fine soft breadcrumbs
- ½ cup (60 g) grated cheese
- 1 dessertspoon chopped parsley
- 1 dessertspoon butter, plus extra for greasing

Mix sweetcorn with beaten eggs, chopped bacon, onion, salt and pepper. Spoon into greased ovenware dish. Cover top with sliced tomatoes.

Mix crumbs, cheese and parsley together. Sprinkle on top of dish. Dot with butter. Bake in moderate (180°C) oven until lightly brown on top and set within.

- **Easy Tomato Tart**
Thaw a sheet of puff pastry. Place on a lined oven tray. Spread pastry with basil or parsley pesto. Slice tomatoes and place on top of pesto. Season generously with cracked black pepper. Bake in a moderate (180°C) oven for approximately 15 minutes. To serve, scatter with chunks of feta cheese and a sprinkling of toasted pine nuts. It's easy to multiply this recipe depending on the number you are feeding for lunch. Each tart will give 4 small pieces. Serve as a side to soup or with a salad for a light lunch.

Tomato Cheese Casserole

SERVES 2

- 4 medium tomatoes, cut into 1 cm slices
- 1 cup (125 g) grated cheddar cheese
- ½ cup (80 g) thinly sliced onion
- ½ teaspoon salt
- pinch of pepper
- 1 cup (35 g) crushed potato chips (crisps)

Arrange half the tomato slices in the bottom of a small casserole. Arrange half the cheese and onion slices in layers over the tomatoes. Sprinkle half the salt and pepper over. Repeat with tomato, then cheese and onion slices. Sprinkle with remainder of salt and pepper. Top with crushed potato chips, bake at 180°C until cheese is melted and bubbly.

Mince Slice

SERVES 4–6

- 1 large carrot
- 1 onion
- 3 potatoes
- 125 g mushrooms
- 1 green capsicum (pepper)
- 1 red capsicum (pepper)
- 500 g lean mince steak
- salt and pepper, to taste
- 1 packet chicken noodle soup
- 1 tablespoon gravy powder
- sheets of shortcrust pastry
- beaten egg or milk, for glaze

Grate carrot, onion and potatoes, finely chop mushrooms and capsicums and add to all the other ingredients, except pastry and glaze. Mix well together.

Line greased slice tin with pastry and press in mixture. Cover with remaining pastry. Glaze with beaten egg and bake at 200°C for 30 minutes. Reduce heat to 180°C and cook for a further 30 minutes.

Savoury Pancakes

SERVES 4

- 1 cup (150 g) self-raising flour
- 1 egg
- ¾ cup (185 ml) milk
- salt and pepper
- butter, for greasing
- grated cheese

FILLING

- 1 onion, peeled and finely chopped
- 1 stick celery, finely chopped
- 1 red capsicum (pepper), finely chopped
- 1 carrot, grated
- a little olive oil, for frying
- 1 cup (230 g) mashed potatoes
- 1 tablespoon milk
- 1 teaspoon chutney
- 2 teaspoons tomato sauce
- salt and pepper

Sift the flour and make a well in the centre. Add the egg and milk and gradually draw in the flour. Beat and stand for 1½–2 hours before using.

Make the pancakes after the standing time. (See page 35 for method.)

For the filling, fry the onion, celery, capsicum and grated carrot in a little olive oil until softened. Combine in a bowl with all the remaining filling ingredients.

Divide the filling evenly among the cooked pancakes, then roll the pancakes up. Place in a greased shallow ovenproof dish, sprinkle with grated cheese, then cook in a moderate (180°C) oven until hot and the cheese has melted and is golden brown.

Chicken and Pumpkin Fritters

MAKES ABOUT 16

- **400 g pumpkin, grated**
- **4 tablespoons olive oil**
- **1 red onion, peeled and finely diced**
- **1–2 cloves garlic, peeled and finely chopped**
- **3 teaspoons garam masala**
- **500 g chicken mince**
- **3 cups (240 g) fresh breadcrumbs**
- **1 cup (30 g) fresh parsley, finely chopped**
- **2 eggs**
- **3 tablespoons plain flour**
- **salt and pepper, to taste**

Place grated pumpkin in a large bowl.

Heat 1 tablespoon oil in a pan and gently fry the onion and garlic until translucent. Add the garam masala and cook 2 minutes, then remove from the heat and cool.

Add the mince, breadcrumbs, parsley, eggs and 2 tablespoons of the flour to the pumpkin along with the cooled onion and mix together. Season with salt and black pepper.

Divide the chicken mixture into about 16 balls, roll in remaining flour. Flatten the balls with your hand. Heat the remaining oil and fry the fritters on medium heat for about 4 minutes each side or until chicken is cooked.

· **Mackerel Fritters**

Tinned mackerel is much cheaper than tinned salmon or tuna. Tip
1 drained tin mackerel into a bowl, mash and add finely chopped fresh
parsley, 2 egg yolks (perhaps left over from making meringues or
pavlova) and 1 cup (150 g) self-raising flour. Mix all together. Form into
little fish cakes, roll in flour and fry gently in hot oil until golden brown.

Chicken Pasta

SERVES 6

- 420 g can creamy chicken and corn soup
- 1 cup (250 ml) pouring cream
- 3 cups (390 g) frozen mixed vegetables
- 375 g cooked pasta
- 1 barbecued chicken, cut into small pieces
- fresh herbs (optional)
- crusty bread, to serve

Heat soup with cream and vegetables. Add pasta
and chicken. Heat through. Top with fresh herbs.
Serve with crusty bread.

Pumpkin, Leek and Spinach Quiche

Serve with a tossed salad. Lovely warm or cold.

SERVES 8

- 400 g pumpkin
- salt and pepper
- olive oil spray or olive oil for drizzling
- olive oil, for frying
- 1 leek, halved lengthways, washed and thinly sliced
- 2 cloves garlic, crushed
- 100 g baby spinach leaves (if you have silverbeet growing in the garden, use that)

- 1 teaspoon grated nutmeg
- 3 rashers bacon (leave out if making vegetarian)
- 4 large eggs
- 2 egg whites
- ¼ cup (60 ml) skim milk
- ¼ cup (60 ml) pouring cream
- 100 g feta cheese
- fresh basil leaves

Preheat oven to 200°C. Line a large baking tray with baking paper.

Peel and cut pumpkin into 2 cm pieces, spread onto baking tray, season with salt and pepper then spray with olive oil spray or drizzle a little oil over the pumpkin. Bake in oven for 30 minutes until soft and golden.

Meanwhile, heat a little olive oil in a pan, add leek and cook, stirring occasionally, for 5 minutes. Add garlic and cook for 1 minute, then stir in the spinach/silverbeet leaves, sprinkle with nutmeg and cook until greens are just wilted. Pour this into a large bowl, then in the same pan quickly cook the bacon till crisp. Add the cooked pumpkin and bacon to the leek and spinach mixture.

Spray a pie dish and spread the pumpkin mixture evenly over the base.

Whisk together the eggs, egg whites, milk and cream and season with salt and pepper. Pour this over the pumpkin mixture, dot with feta cheese and bake in a moderate (180°C) oven for 25 minutes or until puffed and golden. Sprinkle with fresh basil leaves and serve.

Currant Rock Cakes

MAKES ABOUT 60

- 250 g plain flour
- 250 g self-raising flour
- 250 g sugar
- 315 g butter
- 250 g currants
- 2 eggs
- a little milk, if needed

Sift flours, add sugar, rub butter in, add currants, mix to a stiff dough with beaten eggs (may need a little milk). Place on a greased tray in rough balls with forks. Cook in a fairly hot (200°C) oven till golden brown.

Little Sultana Cakes

MAKES 36 PATTY CAKES (RECIPE CAN BE HALVED)

- 1 cup (250 ml) water
- 1 cup (220 g) caster sugar
- 125 g sultanas
- 250 g butter
- 2 teaspoons mixed spice
- 1 teaspoon bicarbonate of soda
- 2 eggs
- 1 cup (150 g) self-raising flour
- 1 cup (150 g) plain flour

In a saucepan, bring the water, sugar, sultanas, butter and mixed spice to the boil. Stir until butter has melted. Take off the heat and add bicarb soda, stirring so it doesn't fizz over the side of the saucepan. Cool this mixture.

When cool, add the beaten eggs and flours. Place into patty pans and bake in a moderate (180°C) oven 12–15 minutes.

Orange Buttermilk Cake

MAKES 1 X 20 CM CAKE

- 1½ cups (225 g) self-raising flour
- 1 cup (220 g) caster sugar
- 2 eggs, lightly beaten
- ½ cup (125 ml) buttermilk (or add a squeeze of lemon juice or 1 dessertspoon white vinegar to 'sour' fresh milk)
- 150 g butter, melted and cooled
- 1½ tablespoons grated orange rind

Lightly grease a 20 cm round cake tin and line with baking paper. Preheat oven to moderate (180°C).

Sift flour into a large bowl, stir in sugar. Make a well in the centre and gradually stir in combined eggs and buttermilk, cooled butter and the rind. Beat till smooth.

Spoon into prepared pan, smooth the top. Bake in oven approximately 40 minutes or until cake is spongy to touch and cake tester comes out clean. Stand in the pan for 5 minutes before turning out onto a cake cooling rack.

Date Slice

SERVES 10

- 125 g butter
- 125 g brown sugar
- ¾ cup (120 g) chopped dates
- ⅓ cup (40 g) chopped walnuts
- 1 cup (150 g) self-raising flour
- 1 egg, beaten
- ½ teaspoon pure vanilla essence
- lemon or chocolate icing

Melt butter in a saucepan, add brown sugar, cook until slightly syrupy. (All sugar does not dissolve, but that is immaterial.)

Combine chopped dates, nuts and flour in a basin, pour on the warm but not hot butter mixture. Lastly add beaten egg and vanilla.

Pour into a slice tin and bake for about 20 minutes in a moderate (180°C) oven, or until golden brown.

Ice with lemon or chocolate icing while slice is still hot. Cool and cut into slices. This slice keeps well in an airtight container.

'Cheese' Cakes

MAKES 12 MINI CAKES

- prepared shortcrust or biscuit pastry
- jam or lemon curd
- 90 g butter
- 3 tablespoons sugar
- ½ teaspoon pure vanilla essence
- 1 egg, beaten
- 1½ cups (225 g) self-raising flour
- salt
- ⅓ cup (80 ml) milk
- icing sugar for dusting

Roll the pastry out thinly and cut into rounds with a floured cutter. Use the rounds to line greased patty tins. Place half a teaspoonful of jam or lemon curd in the bottom of each uncooked pastry case.

Beat the butter and sugar to a soft cream, flavour with the vanilla, and gradually add the beaten egg.

Sift the flour with a pinch of salt and add to the creamed mixture alternately with the milk. Place a spoonful of the cake mixture in each pastry case.

Bake at 180°C for 15 minutes. Remove from tins while hot and dust the tops with sifted icing sugar before serving.

Lemon Loaf

SERVES 8

- 125 g butter
- 1 cup (220 g) caster sugar
- grated rind of 1 large lemon
- 2 well-beaten eggs
- 1½ cups (225 g) self-raising flour
- ¼ teaspoon salt
- ½ cup (125 ml) milk
- juice of 1 lemon mixed with ¼ cup (55 g) caster sugar

Cream butter and sugar together with grated lemon rind. Add eggs.

Sift flour and salt together. Add alternately with milk to mixture.

Bake in loaf tin at 180°C for 30 minutes. When cooked, spoon over the top the juice of the lemon mixed with caster sugar (which has been blended over a gentle heat). Leave to cool in tin.

Zucchini and Walnut Loaves

May be iced with lemon icing, cream cheese icing or left plain and sliced and served buttered. Freezes very well.

MAKES 2 LOAVES

- 2½ cups (375 g) plain flour
- 1½ teaspoons bicarbonate of soda
- 1½ teaspoons baking powder
- 1 teaspoon grated nutmeg
- 1 teaspoon cinnamon
- 1½ cups (330 g) caster sugar
- 1½ cups (210 g) walnuts, chopped
- 1 cup (170 g) sultanas
- 500 g zucchini (courgettes), grated
- 1 cup (250 ml) grapeseed or other light-flavoured oil (not olive oil)
- 3 eggs, beaten

In a large mixing bowl, sift the dry ingredients 3 times, then add all the remaining ingredients and beat well.

Pour into 2 greased and lined loaf tins (you can use 1 loaf tin and 1 ring tin). Bake at 175°C for 45–60 minutes (less in ring tin).

Basic Scone Recipe

MAKES ABOUT 20

- **4 cups (600 g) self-raising flour**
- **a good pinch of salt (for flavour)**
- **300 ml pouring cream**
- **300 ml milk**

Sift flour and salt, then mix all together with cream and milk. Cut out and place on a tray, bake in a hot (220–240°C) oven approximately 12 minutes. When cooked and well risen, the bottom of the scone will sound hollow when tapped.

HINTS FOR MAKING SCONES

- Always treat your scone mixture with a **'light hand'**, don't knead the dough like you do a bread dough.

- 1 tablespoon **cornflour** added to each cup (150 g) of self-raising flour helps to give a light texture to the scone.

- Use a **cold stainless steel knife** to mix as it helps with aeration.

- Dip the **cutter** in flour when cutting out the scones – never twist the cutter or you will end up with 'leaning towers of Pisa'.

- You may need to **vary the amount of liquid** as flours can vary. You need a soft dough not a stiff dough.

- Bake in a **hot** oven.

- When they come out of the oven, **brush off any excess flour** from the outside of the scone (raw flour taste is unpleasant) and wrap in a clean tea towel, which helps to keep them soft.

- **Never cut the scone in half with a knife**. Pull apart with your fingers.

VARIATIONS ON THE BASIC SCONE

- **Fruit Scones**
  Add chopped dates and ginger, or sultanas and currants with
  a sprinkle of mixed spice or cinnamon to the basic mixture.

- **Scone Pizza Base**
  Roll out the scone dough and put on a pizza tray and use as a pizza
  base, top with your favourite pizza toppings.

- **Herb Scones**
  Add finely chopped cooked onions, a sprinkle of mixed dried herbs
  and finely chopped fresh parsley to the basic scone mixture.

- Make into **Savoury Dumplings** by adding finely chopped fresh
  parsley and chives to the basic scone mixture. Roll into small
  balls and drop onto the top of a casserole for the last 15 minutes
  of cooking.

- **Fruit Roly Poly**
  Roll the basic scone mixture quite thinly, spread over any flavour
  jam, some sultanas and peel and grate 2 apples over the mixture,
  roll up like a Swiss roll. Place the roll into a baking dish and pour
  over a syrup made from ½ cup (110 g) sugar, 1 tablespoon butter
  and 1 cup (250 ml) boiling water. Bake in a moderate (180°C) oven
  for 30 minutes. Serve with custard and whipped cream.

- **Scone Swirls**
  Roll out the basic scone mixture, sprinkle with brown sugar,
  cinnamon and sultanas, roll up like a Swiss roll, cut into rounds,
  place face side up in a large greased round cake tin. Bake in a hot
  (200–240°C) oven for 15 minutes. When cool spread with a little icing.

IDEAS FOR SAVOURY SCONES

- **Ham and Cheese Scones**
  Add chopped chives, parsley, some chopped ham, grated cheese and a little chopped red capsicum (pepper) to the basic mixture.

- **Cheese and Gherkin Pinwheels**
  Roll out the scone dough to a 25 cm x 20 cm rectangle. Spread with a jar of gherkin spread and sprinkle with 1½ cups (185 g) grated tasty cheese. Roll up tightly from the long side. Slice into about 16 equal slices and place cut-side up on a lightly floured scone tray and bake.

- **Tomato, Cheese and Onion Pinwheels**
  Fry 1 peeled and finely chopped onion until soft. Roll out the scone dough to a 25 cm x 20 cm rectangle and spread over some tomato paste, top with the cooked onion, sliced tomatoes and sprinkle with some dried mixed herbs to taste and 1½ cups (185 g) grated cheese. Roll up tightly along the long side. Slice into about 16 equal slices. Place on a lightly floured scone tray and bake.

MAIN MEALS

Chicken Schnitzels

SERVES 8

- ½ cup (40 g) fresh breadcrumbs
- ½ cup (30 g) panko breadcrumbs
- 1 tablespoon parsley, finely chopped
- 1 clove garlic, peeled and finely chopped
- 2 tablespoons grated parmesan cheese
- 8 chicken thigh fillets, beaten flat
- flour, for coating
- 1 egg, beaten
- oil, for frying

For the breadcrumb coating mix – combine breadcrumbs and panko breadcrumbs in a bowl, add the parsley, garlic and grated parmesan cheese.

Dust chicken thighs with flour, dip in beaten egg, roll in crumb mixture then fry gently in oil, turning after 5 minutes. Continue frying until chicken is cooked through and crumb coating is crisp and brown.

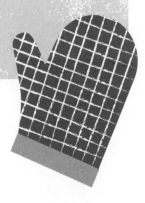

Mum's Chicken Pie

SERVES 4–6

- **butter for greasing**
- **500 g left-over roast chicken, roughly chopped**
- **425 g can condensed chicken or mushroom soup**
- **200 g sliced mushrooms (optional)**
- **½ cup (80 g) frozen peas (optional)**
- **2 sheets frozen shortcrust pastry, thawed**
- **2 tablespoons milk, for brushing**

Heat oven to 180°C and grease a 22 cm pie dish. In a bowl, mix the chicken and enough soup to cover the chicken and vegetables.

Place one sheet of pastry in the pie dish, pour in the chicken mixture. Brush the edges of the pastry with milk. Place the second sheet of pastry on top. Trim to shape and press down the edges with a fork to seal both sheets of pastry together.

Brush top of pie with milk and make a small hole in the centre of the pie to let out steam. Bake for 20 minutes or until lightly coloured.

Note: You can replace a little of the chicken with 2 rashers chopped cooked bacon.

Chicken Nectar

**SERVES 6 ACCOMPANIED
WITH VEGETABLES OF
CHOICE**

- 1 chicken, cut into pieces
- 1 can apricot nectar
- 1 packet French onion soup

Combine all ingredients in a
casserole. Bake in a moderate
(180°C) oven for approximately
1 hour. Serve with rice or
potatoes.

Savoury Chicken Drumsticks

SERVES 4

- 8 chicken drumsticks
- 1 carrot, sliced
- 2 tablespoons plain flour
- 1 teaspoon grated ginger
- ½ teaspoon mustard
- 1 tablespoon sugar
- 1 teaspoon vinegar
- 1 teaspoon soy sauce
- ½ cup (125 ml) tomato sauce
- ½ cup (125 ml) water
- 1 chicken stock cube or
  1 teaspoon chicken stock
  powder
- 1 onion, sliced
- salt and pepper to taste

Place drumsticks in a casserole.
Mix all other ingredients and
pour over chicken. Cook at
180°C for 1½ hours.

Beef and Bean Casserole

SERVES 6–8

- 2 tablespoons butter
- 750 g minced steak
- 1 onion, finely chopped
- ½ teaspoon dried mixed herbs
- 2 teaspoons Worcestershire sauce
- 1 teaspoon chilli powder
- 425 g can tomatoes, drained and chopped
- freshly ground black pepper
- 125 g pasta shells
- 1 cup (125 ml) hot beef stock
- 225 g can baked beans
- parsley, chopped (for garnish)

Melt butter in a saucepan then brown mince and onion. Stir in all remaining ingredients (except for baked beans and parsley). Mix well together and simmer gently for about 30 minutes. When mince is cooked and pasta is tender, stir in baked beans and heat through. Garnish with chopped parsley.

Savoury Mince Pie

SERVES 6–8

- 30 g butter
- 1 kg lean minced steak
- 1 large onion, diced
- 1 large carrot, diced
- 1 small potato, diced
- 1 tablespoon plain flour
- 450 ml water
- ½ cup (125 ml) tomato sauce
- 1 dessertspoon Worcestershire sauce
- 1 tablespoon curry powder
- salt and pepper to taste
- 2 sheets ready-made puff pastry
- beaten egg or milk, for glazing pastry

Heat butter in frying pan, add mince, onion, carrot and potato. Brown mince well and pour off any surplus fat. Stir in flour and mix well. Add water, tomato sauce, Worcestershire sauce, curry powder and salt and pepper. Bring to the boil, cover and simmer for 30 minutes. Allow to cool.

Line a deep 20 cm pie dish with rolled out pastry. Add cold mince mixture, dampen edges and cover with remaining pastry and press edges together. Make two slots in pastry to allow steam to escape. Glaze with egg or milk.

Bake in a 220°C oven for about 15 minutes. Reduce heat to 180°C and bake for a further 20 minutes, until pastry is golden brown. Serve with vegetables and chips.

Chow Mein

SERVES 4

- **500 g lean minced steak**
- **2 onions, chopped**
- **oil, for frying**
- **1 cup (155 g) frozen peas**
- **1 red capsicum (pepper), diced**
- **2 carrots, chopped**
- **3 cups (750 ml) water**
- **3 sticks celery, chopped**
- **2 tablespoons soy sauce**
- **¼ cabbage, shredded**
- **1 tablespoon curry powder**
- **125 g green beans, sliced**
- **1 packet chicken noodle soup**
- **cooked rice or noodles, to serve**

Fry mince and onions in a little oil in a saucepan until brown. Add everything else and simmer for about 30–40 minutes. Serve with cooked rice or noodles.

Lamb Stew with Pumpkin Dumplings

SERVES 4

- 1 teaspoon butter
- 1 medium onion, sliced into rings
- 4 chump chops, cut in half, excess fat removed
- 425 g can whole peeled tomatoes, drained, juice preserved
- ½ cup (125 ml) water
- 3 large mushrooms, halved
- 1 stick celery, cut into 2 cm pieces
- Pumpkin Dumplings (see opposite page)

Melt the butter in a large saucepan. Add the onion and fry for 2 minutes until lightly browned. Add the chops and brown quickly on both sides. Pour the reserved tomato juice and the water into the saucepan, cover and simmer for 15 minutes. Add the tomatoes, mushrooms and celery to the saucepan and push to one side.

Gently place the dumplings on top of the simmering stew, spoon a little juice over, cover tightly and simmer for 20 minutes. Remove the meat, vegetables and dumplings to a serving dish and serve with a little juice spooned over.

Pumpkin Dumplings

Lovely light dumplings that go perfectly
with the lamb stew opposite.

SERVES 4

- ½ cup (75 g) self-raising flour
- 1 tablespoon finely chopped parsley
- 1 teaspoon butter
- ½ cup (125 g) mashed pumpkin

Sift the flour and a pinch of salt into a small bowl.
Add the finely chopped parsley and rub in the butter with
your fingertips. Using a small spatula, add the pumpkin
and mix to form a soft dough. Turn onto a floured board
and knead lightly. Divide the mixture into 4 and
roll each quarter into a ball.

Savoury Chops

SERVES 4

- **4 lamb forequarter chops**
- **butter for greasing**
- **¼ teaspoon each ground ginger, mustard, curry powder and mixed spice**
- **1 cup (250 ml) water, stock or gravy**
- **1 tablespoon sugar**
- **2 tablespoons vinegar**
- **2 tablespoons plain flour**
- **2 tablespoons tomato sauce**
- **salt and pepper, to taste**
- **chopped parsley**

Trim chops and place in buttered casserole dish. Mix remaining ingredients and pour over chops. Leave for 1 hour, then bake for 2 hours in slow (150–160°C) oven. Delicious.

Zucchini and Bacon Pasta Bake

SERVES 4–6

- 3 slices bacon, rind removed and diced
- oil, for frying
- ½ cup (80 g) diced onion
- 2 capsicums (peppers), deseeded and chopped
- 2 zucchini (courgettes), sliced
- ½ teaspoon salt and pepper, or to taste
- ¼ teaspoon dried thyme
- 200 g cooked pasta (penne or macaroni) (100 g uncooked)
- 1 x 400 g tin crushed tomatoes
- ⅔ cup (40 g) panko breadcrumbs
- 1 cup (125 g) grated cheese

Sauté the bacon in a little oil, remove the bacon then sauté the onion in the bacon fat for 5 minutes. Add capsicums and zucchini. Sprinkle with salt, pepper and thyme. Cover and cook over a medium heat for 10–15 minutes, adding the bacon back into the pan for the last 5 minutes of cooking.

Mix in the cooked pasta and tomatoes. If too thick, add a little water or chicken stock. Put into a shallow dish, sprinkle with panko breadcrumbs and grated cheese and cook in a 180°C oven until bubbling.

Apricot Meat Loaf

SERVES 6–8

- 425 g can apricots in natural fruit juice
- butter for greasing
- 2 tablespoons fresh breadcrumbs
- 375 g beef mince
- 2 teaspoons curry powder
- 375 g pork or veal mince
- freshly ground pepper, to taste
- 1 rasher bacon, chopped
- ½ cup (95 g) cooked medium-grain rice
- 2 small eggs
- 1½ tablespoons brown sugar
- 1 teaspoon ground ginger

Preheat oven on 180°C. Drain apricots in a sieve set over a bowl and reserve the juice.

Grease 21 x 19 cm loaf tin with butter and place 10 apricot halves on bottom with cut side up. Chop remaining apricots finely.

Place all remaining ingredients in a bowl (except apricot juice, brown sugar and ginger) and mix with your hands until well combined.

Carefully pack mixture into tin so apricots remain in place. Press down firmly when all the mixture is in place.

Grease a baking dish, place over loaf tin and invert so tin is upside down in dish. Do not remove tin, as loaf is released during cooking.

Cook in a 180°C oven for 30 minutes then remove loaf tin.

Mix ½ of reserved apricot juice with the brown sugar and ginger until sugar has dissolved. Pour over loaf and return to oven for 30 minutes, basting loaf occasionally with dish juices.

Lift onto serving dish and serve with seasonal vegetables.

Slow Cooker Apricot Pork Chops

Pork shoulder chops are more economical than other pork cuts and work well in a slow cooker.

SERVES 4–6

- 6 pork shoulder chops
- 1 brown onion, peeled and finely diced
- 3 cloves garlic, peeled and finely chopped
- 1 packet French onion soup
- 1 tin apricot nectar
- 2 tablespoons soy sauce
- 1 tablespoon cornflour, if needed

Place shoulder chops layered with onion and garlic into the slow cooker. Sprinkle over the French onion soup. Pour over the apricot nectar and soy sauce. Bake on low for 8 hours. If extra thickening is required, mix 1 tablespoon cornflour with a little water and add towards the end of the cooking time to thicken.

Savoury Casserole

SERVES 4

- 1 teaspoon mustard
- 1 teaspoon mixed spice
- 1 teaspoon curry powder
- 2 tablespoons tomato sauce
- 2 tablespoons plain flour
- 1 tablespoon vinegar
- 1 tablespoon sugar
- 1 very finely chopped onion
- salt and pepper to taste
- 600 ml water
- 500 g meat of choice, e.g. chops, sausages, diced steak or chicken

Mix all ingredients, except meat, to a paste.

Pour the mixture over meat and bake at 180°C for 1–1½ hours.

Savoury Golden Sausages

SERVES 6

- 2 tablespoons
  plain flour
- 1 tablespoon sugar
- 1 tablespoon
  Worcestershire sauce
- 2 teaspoons soy sauce
- 2 tablespoons vinegar
- salt and pepper
- 750 g sausages, boiled
  and sliced thickly
- 1 onion, chopped
- 1 grated carrot
- 1 tablespoon chopped
  parsley (optional)

Mix together the flour,
sugar, Worcestershire sauce,
soy sauce and vinegar. Add
1½–2 cups (375–500 ml) water
and some salt and pepper.

Place sausages into casserole.
Add onion, carrot and parsley.
Pour over sauce. Cook in
moderate oven 180°C for
1½ hours.

Serve with boiled rice or
mashed potatoes.

Clayton's Quiche

The Quiche You Have When You're Not Having a Quiche.
Can be served plain or with tomato sauce or with salad.

SERVES 6–8

- 1 cup (220 g) rice
- 1 chopped onion
- 1 cup (150 g) bacon pieces (or more)
- vegetable oil, for frying
- 4 large or 6 small eggs
- ¾ cup (185 ml) milk
- salt and pepper
- 1 teaspoon curry powder

While rice is cooking, sauté onion and bacon in a little oil.

Mix all ingredients together, then put mixture into
a greased shallow pan approximately 14 x 26 cm.
Cook for about 30 minutes in a moderate
(180°C) oven, or until set.

Sweet and Sour Sauce

This keeps well in the refrigerator and may be made into a casserole by the addition of grilled pork sausages, veal, cold lamb or even chicken wings.

USE WITH 1 KG MEAT OF CHOICE

- 1 tin pineapple pieces or crushed pineapple
- 2 tablespoons golden syrup
- 2 large tomatoes, cut into large chunks
- 2 red capsicums (peppers), seeds removed, thinly sliced
- ¾ cup (185 ml) water
- ½ cup (100 g) brown sugar
- 2 teaspoons soy sauce
- salt and pepper, to taste
- ½ cup (125 ml) vinegar or lemon juice, as preferred
- 2–3 tablespoons cornflour

Mix all ingredients, except the cornflour, in a saucepan and bring to boiling point. Cook slowly for 5 minutes, or until capsicum is soft. Thicken with the cornflour mixed with a little extra water.

Salmon Quiche

- 220 g can salmon
- 1 onion, finely chopped
- 3 bacon rashers
- 1 cup (90 g) sliced mushrooms
- oil, for frying
- 1 cup (250 ml) pouring cream
- 3 eggs
- ½ teaspoon salt
- ½ teaspoon paprika
- 2 teaspoons parsley, chopped
- 1 cup (125 g) grated cheese

PASTRY

- 1 cup (150 g) flour
- pinch salt
- ¼ level teaspoon baking powder
- 60 g butter
- 1 tablespoon water/squeeze of lemon juice
- or use 1 sheet of purchased puff pastry, pre-cooked for 8 minutes

For the pastry, sift dry ingredients into a bowl. Rub in butter. Add water/lemon juice to make dough. Roll out pastry and place in a greased 23 cm tin, pressing the pastry into the corners. Top with baking paper, then fill with baking weights or dried beans. Bake at 220°C for 10 minutes. After baking, remove the paper and baking weights or beans.

Sprinkle flaked salmon over pastry base.

Sauté onion, bacon and mushrooms in a little oil, then add on top of salmon. Combine cream, eggs, salt, paprika and parsley and half the cheese and pour into flan. Sprinkle the remaining cheese on top. Bake at 190°C for 30–35 minutes.

Fish Pie

If you have cooked too much fish for a meal, turn it into
a fish pie for dinner the next night.

SERVES 4

- 400 g cooked fish
- 1 onion, peeled and finely diced
- butter or oil, for frying

CHEESE SAUCE
- 2 tablespoons butter
- 2 tablespoons flour
- 2 cups (500 ml) milk
- ground white pepper
- ½ teaspoon Dijon mustard
- ½ cup (60 g) grated cheese

SAVOURY CRUMBLE TOPPING
- 1 cup (60 g) fresh breadcrumbs made from stale bread
- ½ cup (70 g) mixed chopped nuts
- parsley, finely chopped
- 50 g butter, melted

Chop the cooked fish and lay in a pie dish.

Fry the onion in a little butter or oil and add to the fish.

For the cheese sauce, melt the butter, then add the flour to make a 'roux' and cook a little, stirring all the time. Gradually add the milk and whisk till smooth. Season with ground white pepper to taste, add the mustard and grated cheese. Stir until the cheese has melted. Pour over the fish and onion.

For the savoury crumble topping, mix all the dry ingredients together and stir in the butter to make a crumble texture.

Sprinkle the topping over the fish and bake in a 180°C oven until the crumble top is crispy about 20 minutes.

Cod Parmesan

- 100 g macaroni
- salt
- 500 g smoked cod
- 2–3 bay leaves
- few peppercorns
- juice 1 lemon
- 30 g butter
- 30 g flour
- 500 ml milk
- 120 g grated parmesan or tasty cheese
- cayenne pepper, to taste

Cook macaroni in salted water about 15 minutes and drain.

Poach the fish by covering with water and bring to the boil, drain. Cover with fresh water containing 2 or 3 bay leaves, peppercorns and lemon juice, cook gently for 5 minutes, cool and flake.

Make sauce by melting the butter, stirring in the flour and gradually adding the milk. Stir until boiling and cook for 3 minutes. Add half the cheese, then flavour with salt and cayenne pepper.

Place alternate layers of macaroni and fish in a casserole, covering each with sauce and a sprinkle of cheese, finishing with sauce and the last of the cheese. Heat in 180°C oven till cheese is browned.

Fish and Mushroom Crumble

Serve with potatoes sprinkled with parsley,
and steamed fresh vegetables.

- **750 g fish fillets**
- **seasoned flour**
- **oil, for shallow-frying**
- **125 g butter, plus
  1 tablespoon butter
  cut into small pieces**
- **250 g fresh mushrooms,
  chopped roughly**
- **⅔ cup (100 g) plain flour**
- **2 cups (500 ml) milk**
- **salt and pepper**
- **¾ cup (85 g) white
  breadcrumbs**

Dredge fish in seasoned flour and
shallow-fry in oil until flesh flakes,
turning once. Remove and place
in ovenproof dish.

Wipe pan clean and then melt
125 g butter. Add mushrooms and
sauté for 2 minutes. Add flour, stir
well and gradually add milk, stirring
until thickened. Season to taste.

Spread mushroom mixture over
fish fillets and top with breadcrumbs
and the chopped butter. Bake at
190°C until crumbs are golden.

Ann's Salmon or Tuna Slice

SERVES 6

- ready-made shortcrust pastry
- 1 medium brown onion, peeled and finely sliced
- oil, for frying
- cheese sauce (see Fish Pie recipe, page 103)
- 3 or 4 rashers of bacon, chopped, fat removed, lightly cooked in the microwave for 90 seconds
- 180 g can salmon or tuna
- 3 lightly beaten eggs
- salt and pepper, to taste
- finely chopped parsley
- slices of tomato (optional)
- beaten egg white, for glazing
- grated cheese, for topping

Grease and line an 18 x 28 cm slice pan or equivalent pan with pastry, taking the pastry halfway up the sides of the pan if it is deep. (If using sheets of frozen pastry then make in a shallow 22 cm square tin the size of the pastry sheets.)

Lightly fry the onion in the oil.

Cover the pastry base with cheese sauce. Sprinkle with the chopped bacon and onion.

Drain and break up the salmon or tuna (remove bones from tin of salmon if using). Combine the lightly beaten eggs with the salmon or tuna, add salt and pepper if required and the parsley. Pour into the slice pan and top with the tomato (optional). Cover with more pastry, glaze with beaten egg white, sprinkle with grated cheese and bake at 180°C for approximately 30 minutes.

Savoury Tuna Slice

SERVES 6

- 2 eggs
- 1 cup (250 ml) milk
- 425 g can tuna (add more if you wish)
- 2 cups (250 g) grated tasty cheese
- 1 cup (100 g) crushed dry biscuits such as Savoy or Jatz (crush a few biscuits at a time until you have filled a cup)
- ¼ cup (40 g) finely chopped spring onions or chives
- ½ cup (30 g) finely chopped parsley

Beat eggs, add milk, then all other ingredients, except parsley, mixing well.

Line a slice tray (not too large) with greased foil. Spread mixture into tray. Cook ½ hour in moderate (180°C) oven (or until golden brown).

When cool, cut into squares or fingers. Garnish with parsley. Can be served hot or cold.

Red Salmon Cheese Cake

SERVES 6–8

- melted butter, for brushing
- 125 g crushed dried biscuits
- 60 g butter
- 250 g cream cheese
- 300 ml pouring cream
- 3 eggs, lightly beaten
- 415 g tin red salmon, drained and flaked
- 4 French shallots, finely chopped
- rind 1 lemon, finely grated
- 250 g cottage cheese

Preheat oven to 180°C. Brush a deep 23 cm springform tin with melted butter.

Place biscuit crumbs into a bowl, add butter and mix well. Spread in tin and press down well. Chill in freezer.

Mix cream cheese, cream and eggs very well. Fold in salmon, shallots, rind and season with salt and pepper to taste. Add cottage cheese last. Spoon into tin, smooth top and bake 55–60 minutes at 180°C. Test to see if centre is set.

Impossible Salmon Pie

SERVES 6

- 4 eggs
- 125 g softened butter
- ½ cup (75 g) plain flour
- ½ teaspoon baking powder
- 2 cups (500 ml) milk
- 1 x 200 g can salmon, drained and flaked
- 1 onion, peeled and finely chopped
- ¼ red capsicum (pepper), finely chopped
- ½ cup (60 g) grated cheese
- ⅓ cup (20 g) finely chopped parsley
- salt and pepper, to taste

Place eggs, butter, flour and baking powder in food processor bowl and process until smooth. Transfer to a bowl and stir in the milk, salmon, onion, capsicum, cheese, parsley, salt and pepper.

Pour mixture into a greased 25 cm pie plate or quiche dish. Bake in a moderate (180°C) oven for approximately 45–60 minutes until mixture is firm to touch and golden.

Can be served hot or cold with salad.

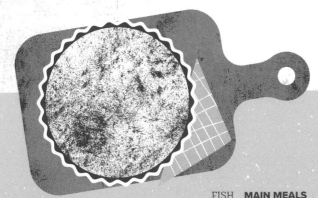

Red Salmon Potato Bake

SERVES 12

- 8 medium potatoes
- 20 g butter, plus extra for greasing
- 2 leeks
- 3 eggs
- 300 g light sour cream
- 300 ml pouring cream
- salt and pepper, to taste
- ¼ cup (15 g) chopped chives (or chopped fresh dill)
- 2 x 415 g cans red salmon
- 1 medium zucchini (courgette), very thinly sliced
- 1 cup (125 g) grated tasty cheese
- sweet paprika

Peel and cook potatoes until tender. Drain, cool and cut into thick slices.

Melt butter in a pan and add finely chopped leeks and cook till soft. Set aside.

Combine eggs, sour cream and pouring cream in a jug. Season well with salt and pepper.

In an 18 cm x 30 cm greased ovenproof pan, place a layer of potato, sprinkle with half the chives and cooked leeks, then half the salmon. Repeat layers, then pour the cream mixture over the top. Lay zucchini slices on top, sprinkle with grated cheese, then the paprika.

Cook, uncovered, in a moderate (180°C) oven for about 45–60 minutes until browned and the egg mixture is set. Allow to stand for 10 minutes before cutting.

Salmon with Capsicum Sauce

SERVES 4

- **1 small red chilli, seeded and chopped**
- **2 cloves garlic, crushed**
- **1 red capsicum, seeded and diced**
- **3 tablespoons vegetable oil**
- **2 tablespoons brown sugar**
- **1 tablespoon rice vinegar**
- **1 tablespoon soy sauce**
- **250 ml water**
- **2 teaspoons cornflour combined with 1 tablespoon water and 2 teaspoons lemon juice**
- **180 g egg noodles**
- **3 teaspoons sesame oil**
- **1 tablespoon lime juice**
- **2 tablespoons chopped fresh coriander**
- **4 salmon fillets**

Sauté chilli, garlic and capsicum in 1 tablespoon of the oil, stirring occasionally until capsicum is softened, about 3 minutes. Stir in sugar, vinegar, soy sauce and water; reduce heat to low and cook for 5 minutes. Stir in the cornflour, water and lemon mixture, and bring to boil. Cook to thicken. Remove from heat.

Cook noodles as directed on packet, then drain.

In small bowl, combine sesame oil, lime juice and coriander. Mix well. Pour over noodles and toss to coat.

In pan over medium–high heat, warm the remaining 2 tablespoons vegetable oil and add salmon fillets. Cook until fish flakes easily when tested with a fork (2–3 minutes per side).

To serve, reheat sauce, arrange noodles and salmon fillets on individual plates. Spoon sauce on top and serve immediately.

Macaroni Fish En Casserole

SERVES 4

- 400 g cooked white fish such as flake
- 1 teaspoon salt
- 2 tablespoons melted butter, plus extra for greasing and dotting on top of casserole
- 3 tablespoons grated cheese
- 1 teaspoon chopped onion
- 1 x 440 ml can tomato soup diluted with ½ cup (125 ml) water
- 80 g macaroni, cooked according to packet instructions
- 3 hard-boiled eggs
- breadcrumbs, to cover

Flake fish with fork, add salt, butter, cheese, onion and tomato soup. Add macaroni and mix thoroughly.

Slice eggs, and arrange fish mixture and eggs alternately in a deep, buttered dish. Cover with breadcrumbs and dot with butter.

Bake in moderate (180°C) oven until top is nicely brown and mixture thoroughly hot, approximately ½ hour.

Chickpea and Potato Curry

SERVES 4

- 1 tablespoon oil
- 2 tablespoons curry powder
- 1 tablespoon black mustard seeds
- 500 g orange sweet potato, chopped
- 1 cup (250 ml) vegetable stock (or water and a vegetable stock cube)
- 2 x 425 g cans chickpeas, drained
- 440 g can tomatoes, chopped

Heat oil in a wok. Add curry powder and mustard seeds, cook until seeds pop and curry is fragrant. Add sweet potato and vegetable stock and cook covered, for 10 minutes. Add the rest of the ingredients and cook uncovered, for 4–5 minutes.

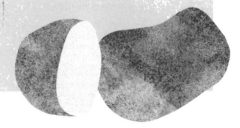

Curried Egg and Cheese Casserole

SERVES 4

- 4 eggs
- 45 g white rice
- 1 small onion
- 1 small apple
- 1 small tomato
- 1 tablespoon butter
- 1 dessertspoon flour
- 1 teaspoon curry powder
- pepper and salt, to taste
- 1 teaspoon desiccated coconut
- 300 ml stock or water
- 15 g currants or sultanas
- a few drops lemon juice
- 2 tablespoons finely chopped parsley

Boil eggs 15 minutes. Place in cold water and remove shells. Quarter and set aside. Boil rice 15 minutes in plenty of salted water, drain well. Set aside.

Peel and chop the onion and apple. Finely chop the tomato.

Melt butter, fry onion and apple till brown, add tomato, fry again. Add flour, curry powder, pepper, salt and coconut, stir till well browned. Add stock, stir till it boils and thickens, add rice then the quartered hard boiled eggs and remaining ingredients.

Pour into a casserole, and top with the savoury cheese topping – see opposite page for how to finish.

Savoury Cheese Topping

- 60g flour
- ¼ teaspoon salt
- 60g butter
- 300 ml milk
- 3 eggs, separated
- ¼ teaspoon Worcestershire sauce
- 1 cup (125 g) grated cheese

Sift flour and salt. Melt butter in a saucepan, add sifted ingredients, stir till smooth, cook 1 minute. Add milk, cook, stirring till thick. Cool. Beat in egg yolks, sauce and cheese. Taste, add more sauce if liked.

Whip egg whites stiffly, and fold into mixture.

Place on top of curried eggs in casserole dish. Place the casserole dish in a large baking dish. Pour in hot water to halfway up the sides of the casserole, and bake in a moderate oven (180°C) for around 30 minutes.

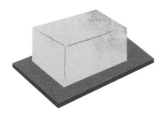

Mixed Vegetable Stir-fry

SERVES 2

- 2 cloves garlic, crushed
- 1 leek, washed and sliced
- 2 stalks celery, sliced
- 2 carrots, sliced thinly diagonally
- 1 capsicum (pepper), sliced
- oil, for frying
- 2 bok choy, sliced
- 100 g snow peas (mange tout)
- ½ cup (125 ml) vegetable stock

Sauté garlic, leek, celery, carrots and capsicum
in a little oil in a non-stick wok.
Add bok choy and snow peas.

Add vegetable stock. Cook 2 minutes. Remove
from heat. Serve with rice (or meat), or eat
unaccompanied.

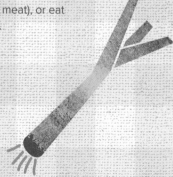

Medley Pie with Onion Biscuit Topping

SERVES 4

- ¼ cup (60 g) butter
- or olive oil
- 1 onion, finely diced
- 1 x 440 g can kidney beans, drained
- 1 x 440 g can baked beans
- ¼ cup (35 g) plain flour
- salt and pepper, to taste
- 1½ cups (375 ml) water
- ½ cup (80 g) cooked peas
- ¼ cup (25 g) carrots, diced
- ½ cup (55 g) pearl onions
- Onion Biscuit Topping
- 1 cup (150 g) plain flour
- pinch salt
- ¼ teaspoon baking powder
- ½ cup (125 g) butter
- 1 egg yolk
- 2 tablespoons vegetable stock
- 1 dessertspoon grated cheese

Melt the butter in a pan, add chopped onion and cook till golden brown. Reserve half for biscuit topping. Add beans and stir in plain flour. Season with salt and pepper and add water. Stir until boiling and cook for 10 minutes.

Place half in a pie dish, cover with peas, carrot and pearl onions, then add remainder of beans. Allow to cool while making the biscuit topping.

Sift flour, salt and baking powder. Rub in the butter and add the reserved onion.

Beat egg yolk with the stock and mix to a dry dough. Turn onto a floured board and roll to fit pie dish. Pinch a frill round the edge, brush the surface with milk and sprinkle with cheese. With a sharp scissors, snick pastry in the centre to allow steam to escape. Bake in upper part of 180–200°C oven for 12–15 minutes.

Curry Vegetables

Suggested vegetables to use: runner beans, peas, potatoes, cauliflower, tomatoes. The garlic, ginger and cumin optional, but they do help to give that extra taste.

SERVES 4

- **375 g onions, chopped fine**
- **cooking margarine**
- **1 teaspoon curry powder**
- **2–3 bay leaves**
- **¼ teaspoon turmeric**
- **250 g tomatoes, chopped**
- **chopped parsley**
- **2 cloves of garlic, chopped fine**
- **small piece of ginger, chopped fine**
- **¼ teaspoon ground cumin**
- **500 g chopped mixed vegetables and potatoes**

Fry onions in margarine. When onions are golden brown, add curry powder, bay leaves, turmeric, tomatoes, parsley, garlic, ginger and cumin. Keep on stirring, then add the vegetables and a little water and keep stirring till vegetables are cooked.

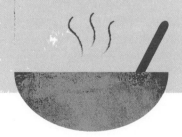

Meatless Chilli

SERVES 4

- 2 tablespoons oil
- ½ cup (110 g) pearl barley
- 2¼ cups (560 ml) water
- 1 cup (220 g) quick-cooking brown rice
- 1 tablespoon chilli powder
- 1 x 425 g can tomato puree
- 1 x 400 g can tomatoes with juice
- 1 x 420 g can red kidney beans, drained and rinsed
- 300 g frozen corn kernels, thawed and drained
- ¼ teaspoon cayenne pepper
- 90 g grated cheese
- 2 tablespoons pumpkin seeds (optional)

Heat the oil in a large saucepan over moderate heat for 1 minute. Stir in the barley and cook, stirring often, for 2 minutes. Add the water, bring to a boil, and cook for 15 minutes. Add the rice and chilli powder. Return to a boil, cover, and cook for 5 minutes.

Stir in the tomato puree, tomatoes, beans, corn kernels and cayenne pepper, and bring to a boil again. Simmer for 10 minutes or until the rice and barley are tender. Sprinkle each serving with the cheese and the pumpkin seeds.

Caramelled Apple Pudding

This is a variation of the common apple pie.

SERVES 4–6

- 3 or 4 peeled, cored cooking apples, such as granny smith, stewed with a minimal amount of water
- 1 cup (250 ml) hot water
- juice 1 lemon
- ½ cup (115 g) caster sugar
- 1 tablespoon butter

PASTRY
- 60 g butter
- 125 g flour
- pinch salt
- water

Make a plain pastry – rub butter into flour and salt. Add enough cold water to make pastry.

Roll out pastry and cover with unsweetened stewed apple. Roll up like Swiss roll and place in greased dish.

Into a saucepan, put the hot water, lemon juice, sugar and butter. Bring to boil and then pour over the apple roll. Bake in a moderate (180°C) oven for about 35–40 minutes. Serve with cream or ice cream.

Plum Sago Pudding

SERVES 4–6

- **2 large tablespoons sago**
- **½ cup (125 ml) milk (enough milk to cover sago)**
- **1 teaspoon bicarbonate of soda**
- **½ cup (115 g) caster sugar**
- **1 teaspoon mixed spice**
- **1 cup (125 g) sultanas or raisins**
- **2 tablespoons butter**
- **1 large cup (110 g) breadcrumbs**
- **pinch salt**

Soak sago in enough milk to cover it, overnight.

Next day, dissolve soda into the milk and sago.

Mix all ingredients in a basin and add the milk and sago mixture. Mix well, place in a greased pudding steamer and steam for 3 hours.

Apple–Rice Fluff

SERVES 4

- 2 cups (400 g) hot cooked tart apples, e.g. granny smith (about 5 or 6 apples peeled, cored and cooked)
- ½ cup (115 g) caster sugar
- 1½ teaspoons lemon juice
- 1 cup (185 g) cooked white rice (see note)
- 1 cup (120 g) whipped cream
- cinnamon, to garnish

Mash hot apples, add sugar and lemon juice, then rice. Cool thoroughly.

Fold the whipped cream into the apple–rice mixture. Place in dessert dishes and chill. Garnish with cinnamon.

Note: To get 1 cup cooked rice, use ½ cup/100 g raw rice.

Butterscotch Self-saucing Pudding

SERVES 4

- 1 cup (150 g) self-raising flour
- ¾ cup (170 g) caster sugar
- ½ teaspoon salt
- 60 g butter, melted
- ½ cup (125 ml) milk
- 1 egg

FOR THE SAUCE

- 2 tablespoons golden syrup
- 1½ cups (375 ml) hot water
- 30 g butter

To make the sauce, place all ingredients in saucepan and stir until butter melts.

Mix all ingredients for the pudding well, place in a greased ovenproof dish and pour the sauce over the top of mixture. Bake in moderate (180°C) oven 30–35 minutes.

Chocolate Bread Pudding

SERVES 4

- 2 cups (500 ml) milk, plus extra if needed
- 1 cup (80 g) fresh breadcrumbs
- 2 tablespoons butter
- salt
- pure vanilla essence, if liked
- 1 tablespoon cocoa
- 3 eggs, separated
- 2 tablespoons caster sugar, plus 2 extra tablespoons for meringue
- apricot jam or whatever jam you prefer

Heat milk, add breadcrumbs, butter, salt and vanilla.

Mix cocoa in a little milk and add to warm milk mixture.

Beat egg yolks and sugar, add to milk. Pour into a pie dish, stand dish in a dish of cold water and bake in a moderate (180°C) oven for approximately 25 minutes or until custard is just set. Spread with apricot jam or any other kind you like.

Make a meringue with the egg whites and extra sugar, pile onto pudding, put back in cool oven to set the meringue.

Lemon Dumplings

SERVES 4–6

- 3 tablespoons butter
- 2 cups (300 g) self-raising flour
- pinch salt
- a little milk, as needed
- 3 cups (750 ml) water
- 1 small cup (210 g) caster sugar
- juice of 2 lemons
- 2 large tablespoons golden syrup

Rub butter into flour and salt. Mix to a dough with a little milk.

Boil water, sugar, lemon juice and golden syrup for 1 minute. Pop in dough, which has been divided into pieces, and boil 20 minutes.

COOKING FOR A CROWD:
SAVOURY AND SWEET

THRIFTY SANDWICH TIPS FOR A CROWD

- If you are pre-slicing **tomatoes** ready to make a large quantity of sandwiches, place the crusts from loaves of bread in the bottom of containers to soak up the juice to save soggy sandwiches.

- Vertically cut **tomatoes** keep their shape better.

- Place folded paper towel in the bottom of a container or on a plate to drain and dry **beetroot** before placing on a plate of salad or in a sandwich. This will soak up the juice to prevent sogginess or beetroot juice spreading over the salad.

- When making **egg filling** for sandwiches, instead of mixing the cooked, shelled hard-boiled eggs with only mayonnaise, which can leave a harsh flavour, mix in a little pouring cream or melted butter with the mayonnaise. Very finely chopped parsley, chives OR a little curry powder added to the egg mixture, gives extra flavour. (The fresher the egg, the harder they are to peel once hard-boiled. As the egg ages, the membrane just under the shell comes away from the egg easier.)

- Crack the shells of **hard-boiled eggs** immediately to stop the cooking process and cool down quickly in cold water.

- As a rule of thumb, a **single loaf of bread** yields approximately 20 slices. You will need about 125 g butter to cover all the slices. Allow 1½ rounds sandwiches per person.

- To **make the butter go further**, beat 125 g butter until soft, then gradually add 4 tablespoons milk with 1 teaspoon of gelatine dissolved in the milk whilst beating, adding salt if required. This is the equivalent of 250 g butter.

Mock Chicken Sandwich Filling

Mock chicken (or 'mock turkey') is a tasty and cheap sandwich spread. This makes enough for sandwiches from 1 loaf of sliced bread.

- 1 onion
- 3 large tomatoes
- 120 g grated cheese
- 120 g butter
- 1½ teaspoons mixed herbs
- 4 tablespoons fresh breadcrumbs

Peel and finely dice the onion. Finely chop the tomatoes.

Simmer all ingredients (except breadcrumbs) gently for 10 minutes. When cooked, add breadcrumbs.

THRIFTY SALAD TIPS FOR A CROWD

- To provide **2 tablespoons of salad per head for 50 people**, allow about 4 kg total of salad.

- If **pre-preparing lettuce** for the next day, place a stainless steel knife or fork in the bowl with the cut up lettuce, cover with cold water and store in the fridge. It will keep the lettuce crisp and fresh.

- **French Salad**
  One large bowl of mixed lettuce goes a long way. Make sure lettuce is washed and spun dry or dried by being wrapped in a clean towel. Just before serving, mix through 3–4 peeled and chopped avocados (if in season and cheap, otherwise use peeled and sliced cucumber) and finish with French Dressing (see page 134). Once dressing has been added to the salad, it becomes soggy if not used on the day of making.

Coleslaw

SERVES 50

- **1 kg cabbage, chopped (whatever you have on hand or a mixture of varieties is always nice – some red cabbage, some green savoy)**
- **500 g finely sliced Chinese cabbage (wong bok)**
- **1 kg carrots, peeled and grated**
- **750 g red capsicums (peppers), or a mixture of coloured capsicums, cut in half, membrane and seeds removed and finely chopped**
- **500 g finely sliced celery**
- **1 red onion, finely diced (optional)**
- **220 g can pineapple pieces, well drained, OR 200 g apples, unpeeled and cut into fine slivers**

DRESSING
- **3 cups (750 g) each mayonnaise and sour cream or plain yoghurt**

Beat the dressing ingredients together. Pour the dressing into the chopped and sliced vegetables – do it in stages as you may not need the full quantity of dressing.

If there's any dressing left over, store it in a glass jar in the fridge.

Rice Salad

SERVES 50

- 1.5 kg rice, either brown or white, cooked and cooled
- 1 kg red capsicums (peppers), cut in half, seeds and membrane removed and finely diced
- 1 kg corn, canned, or cook the equivalent in fresh corn
- 3 cups (450 g) currants
- 1 bunch spring onions, finely sliced (optional)
- chopped celery or red onion (optional)

DRESSING

- 500 ml light-flavoured oil, such as sunflower or grapeseed oil
- 150 ml lemon juice
- salt and ground white pepper, to taste
- 5 cloves garlic, peeled and crushed

Mix the dressing ingredients together until well combined. You may not need this amount of dressing but any left over will keep well in the fridge.

Combine the dressing with the salad ingredients.

Note: 100 ml soy sauce (or to taste) added to the dressing makes a nice flavour change.

Potato Salad

SERVES 50

- 5 kg waxy potatoes (e.g. Desiree variety)
- 1 bunch parsley, finely chopped
- 12 eggs, hard-boiled and peeled
- 2 bunches chives, finely chopped
- 6 rashers bacon, diced and cooked
- salt
- ground white pepper

DRESSING

- 3 cups (750 g) each mayonnaise and sour cream
- 3 teaspoons seeded mustard

Scrub the potatoes well and peel if using 'old' potatoes or if you don't like the flavour or texture of potato peel. Cook until only just soft. Don't overcook.

Mix the dressing ingredients together well.

Combine the dressing and other ingredients and add salt and ground white pepper to taste. Mix all together well.

Note: 500 g frozen peas, cooked and cooled, make a nice addition and make the salad go further.

Bean Salad

SERVES 50

- 3.5 kg beans in total, e.g. 1.5 kg fresh green beans and
  500 g broad beans (steamed and double-peeled if beans are large)
- 1 kg tinned mixed beans
- optional additions: 500 g cherry tomatoes, halved and 6 rashers
  bacon, chopped and cooked

FRENCH DRESSING
- olive oil
- white wine vinegar
- salt
- ground white pepper
- Dijon mustard, to taste

For the dressing, make up the quantity required (about 4–6 cups/
1–1.5 litres) in the proportions of 3 parts olive oil to 1 part white wine
vinegar. Season with salt and ground white pepper to taste and beat
together until well emulsified, adding the Dijon mustard.

(A purchased balsamic dressing is delicious too.)

Combine the dressing with the salad ingredients.

Waldorf Salad

SERVES 50

- **3.5 kg apples — any variety of apple is suitable but a mixture of red-skinned and green-skinned apples is attractive**
- **juice of 1–2 lemons**
- **2 kg celery, finely diced**
- **250 g walnuts, chopped**
- **4–6 cups (1–1.5 litres) French dressing (see dressing for Bean Salad, opposite, but leave out the mustard)**

Core and quarter the apples and chop into chunks or batons. Leave apples unpeeled. To prevent apples from browning when making the salad, drop chopped pieces into cold water with the juice of 1 or 2 lemons added. Drain well before adding to the other salad ingredients and mixing well to combine.

Green Bean and Cherry Tomato Salad

SERVES 6 (SEE NOTE TO SERVE 50)

- 500 g fresh green beans
- 1 punnet (250 g) cherry tomatoes, or any type of tomato if you have them growing
- ½ bunch spring onions, or use chives if you have them growing
- 2 tablespoons toasted sesame seeds

DRESSING
- 3 tablespoons olive oil
- 2 tablespoons balsamic vinegar
- 1 teaspoon Dijon mustard
- ½ teaspoon sesame oil
- salt and pepper, to taste

Whisk all the dressing ingredients together.

Top and tail beans, and halve if large. Slice tomatoes and spring onions.

Blanch beans in boiling salted water until just tender. Refresh under cold running water, drain well.

Arrange beans, tomatoes and spring onion on a platter, drizzle with dressing and sprinkle toasted sesame seeds on top.

Note: To serve 50 you will need 3.5 kg fresh green beans, 3 bunches finely sliced spring onions and 3 kg halved cherry tomatoes. Make 8 x the quantity of dressing, or use the French dressing recipe for Bean Salad on page 134.

THRIFTY MEAT COOKING TIPS FOR A CROWD

- **Casseroles, curries and pasta bakes** are economical dishes to feed a large number as they use the cheaper cuts of meat.

- **For 50 people, allow 7.5 kg meat** of any sort (without bone in), allowing 125 g meat per person plus a bit extra. To make the casserole or curry go even further (and add nutritional value), add plenty of vegetables as well as tinned lentils and/or beans.

- For a **cold meat platter for 50**, allow approximately 3 kg of various cold cut meats such as sliced ham, corned beef and roast lamb. Allow approximately 6–7 sliced breadsticks for 50 people.

- When **scaling up a recipe**, allow extra cooking time but cook at temperature listed in the recipe – do not cook at a higher heat. When cooking a large amount in a curry or casserole, it is always better to cook longer and slower than try to hurry the cooking process.

- Tinned or dried **lentils** can be added to curries, casseroles, stews and soups. Rinse both tinned and dried before using. They can also be added to shepherd's pie, lasagne or stuffed capsicums (peppers) to extend meat.

- The best way to cook lentils is to boil them – follow packet instructions.

- The liquid from canned chickpeas can be used as an **egg white substitute** to make meringue. Add ⅛ teaspoon cream of tartar to help it to whip.

Simple Lamb Curry

SERVES 50

- 7.5 kg boned lamb shoulder, cut into 2.5 cm chunks
- flour, for coating
- salt and pepper
- 10 brown onions, peeled and sliced
- 12 garlic cloves, peeled and crushed
- 3 tablespoons brown sugar
- 1–3 tablespoons curry powder, or to taste
- 120 g fruit chutney
- 3 x 400 g cans crushed tomatoes
- 2 tablespoons tomato paste
- 7 cups (1.75 litres) chicken stock
- cornflour, if needed

Roll meat in the flour seasoned with salt and pepper. When cooking this volume of ingredients it is not practical to go to the trouble of browning that volume of meat in batches. Combine all ingredients, except cornflour, in a very large bowl. Divide the mixture evenly between 3 large casserole dishes with lids.

Bake in a slow (150–160°C) oven for 2½ hours. Chill overnight to allow the flavours to develop.

Next day, remove any fat that has set on the top and reheat in a slow oven 1½ hours until piping hot. If mixture is not thick enough, mix some cornflour to a paste in water and thicken the curry. Alternatively, you can cook in 2 large slow cookers on low for 8 hours.

Pasta Bake

SERVES 50

- 4 x 500 g packets dried penne
- 10 medium brown onions
- 15 cloves garlic
- 18 rashers bacon (leave out if making a vegetarian pasta bake)
- oil and butter, for frying
- 1.5 kg mushrooms
- 500 g spinach leaves
- Cheese Sauce for Pasta Bake (see page 140)
- 1 packet (200 g) panko breadcrumbs
- 500 g grated cheese

Cook penne according to packet instructions.

Meanwhile peel and chop onions and garlic, and chop bacon into pieces. Fry onions, garlic and bacon in batches in a little olive oil. Finely slice mushrooms and fry in a little butter or olive oil, adding chopped spinach last just to wilt it. Combine all the ingredients.

Spread this mixture into shallow baking dishes or foil trays. Pour over cheese sauce, mix into pasta mixture gently, cover top with panko breadcrumbs and sprinkle with grated cheese. Heat in the oven (160°C) about 20 minutes until bubbling hot and breadcrumb cheese topping has crisped up.

Cheese Sauce for Basic Pasta Bake

This sauce is designed to go with the Pasta Bake recipe on page 139.

SERVES 50

- **240 g butter**
- **200 g plain flour**
- **4.5 litres milk**
- **6 teaspoons Dijon mustard**
- **6 teaspoons Vegeta vegetable stock powder**
- **6 cups (750 g) grated cheese**

It is best to do cheese sauce in batches so that the large volume of milk doesn't catch on the bottom of the saucepan. If doing it all at once make sure you keep stirring continuously, so the milk doesn't catch, and cook slowly.

Melt butter, add flour to make a roux, gradually beat in the milk and keep stirring until mixture is smooth and thickening. Add mustard, stock powder and grated cheese and keep stirring until mixture has thickened.

This is a basic pasta bake – now let your imagination use up what you have in your pantry or fridge. See the optional extras on opposite page.

OPTIONAL EXTRAS

- Add 1.8 kg cooked chopped chicken OR
- Diced left-over cooked pumpkin or sweet potato OR
- Use 6 large cans salmon or tuna OR
- Add grated zucchini (courgette) and roasted red capsicum (pepper) OR
- Use leek instead of onion, or half leek and half onion OR
- Add cooked broccoli instead of spinach OR
- Add finely chopped herbs for extra flavour – dill with a salmon or tuna pasta bake OR parsley, chives or tarragon with a chicken pasta bake OR
- Add 6 chopped deseeded chillies OR
- Alternative base – instead of cheese sauce use 6 litres tomato passata and add cherry tomatoes cut in half.

Beef and Vegetable Casserole

SERVES 50

- **7.5 kg chuck steak (most economical, cheapest cut but needs long slow cooking), diced**
- **plain flour, for coating**
- **salt and pepper**
- **oil, for frying**
- **7 medium brown onions, peeled and sliced**
- **10 carrots, peeled and sliced**
- **12 sticks celery, sliced**
- **7 cups (1.75 litres) beef or vegetable stock**
- **3 x 400 g cans crushed tomatoes**
- **120 ml soy sauce**
- **120 ml Worcestershire sauce**
- **1 tablespoon relish – tomato, zucchini (courgette) or plum**
- **mustard powder or curry powder (optional)**
- **a little cornflour mixed with water, to thicken, if needed**

Roll the meat in plain flour seasoned with salt and pepper. Fry in batches in a little oil if you wish, but to save time just mix together all the ingredients, put into covered casserole dishes and bake for 2–3 hours in a slow (150–160°C) oven.

If using slow cookers, cook on low for 8 hours.

Before serving, taste for flavour, and add more salt and pepper, or tomato relish and Worcestershire sauce according to your taste. Dry mustard or a little curry powder also add extra flavour. Thicken with the cornflour paste if necessary.

Note: To make this go further, add more vegetables, e.g. sliced parsnips, diced pumpkin and sweet potato and sliced zucchini (courgettes). Or add drained cans of cooked beans.

Mum's Beef Stroganoff

SERVES 12 (MULTIPLY BY 4 TO SERVE 50)

- 2 kg round or skirt steak
- 2 brown onions
- 3 tablespoons plain flour
- salt and pepper
- olive oil, for frying
- 1 can cream of mushroom soup
- 2 cans tomato soup
- 2 teaspoons Tabasco sauce
- 3 tablespoons Worcerstershire sauce
- 200 g fresh mushrooms, sliced
- 1 carton (300 g) sour cream

Dice steak and peel and slice onions. Roll diced steak in flour seasoned with salt and pepper to taste.

Brown steak in a little olive oil in a heavy-bottomed casserole dish in batches, adding a little more oil as needed. Remove all steak. Add a little more oil and brown onions. Put steak back into the pot, add all other ingredients, except sour cream, and stir to mix well.

Bake in a slow oven (150–160°C) about 2 hours or in the slow cooker on low for 8 hours. Before serving, pour in one container of sour cream and mix well and reheat if necessary.

Serve on a bed of cooked fettuccine and with a green vegetable on the side.

Savoury Sausages

Can easily be multiplied to feed the number you are catering for.

SERVES 8 (MULTIPLY BY 6 TO SERVE 50)

- 1 kg thin plain beef sausages (there are about 15 thin sausages to the kilo)
- 1 brown onion
- 2 sticks celery
- 2 carrots
- 1 tablespoon oil
- 1 zucchini (courgette), sliced
- 2 rashers bacon, diced
- 3 teaspoons ground coriander
- ½ cup (125 g) tomato relish
- 1 tablespoon Dijon mustard
- 2 tablespoons Worcerstershire sauce
- 1 cup (250 ml) chicken stock or 1 cup (250 ml) water with 1 teaspoon stock powder
- 2 silverbeet leaves, including the stalks
- a little tomato passata, if needed

Boil the sausages for 5 minutes to par-cook. When cool enough to handle, cut each sausage into 4 pieces.

Peel and finely dice onion, celery and carrots. Heat the oil in a heavy-based pot and gently cook the carrot, celery, zucchini and onion until soft. Add the diced bacon and cook another few minutes. Add all other ingredients and the sausages and continue to cook until vegetables are cooked through. If mixture becomes too dry, add a little tomato passata or chicken stock.

Serve with mashed potato or cooked rice.

Apricot Chicken with Vegetables

SERVES 10 (MULTIPLY BY 5 TO SERVE 50)

- 2 onions
- 3 carrots
- 3 sticks celery
- 2 kg chicken thigh fillets, skin off
- oil, for frying
- 2 rashers bacon, diced
- 2 x 400 ml tins apricot nectar
- 2 packets French onion soup
- 3 tablespoons soy sauce
- 1 tablespoon cornflour, if needed

Peel and finely dice onion and carrots. Finely chop celery. Dice chicken thighs into bite-sized pieces.

Heat a little oil in a heavy-based pot. Gently cook the onion, carrots and celery until they are soft, add diced bacon and continue cooking for another few minutes. Add all other ingredients and cook until the chicken is cooked. If needed, thicken with 1 tablespoon cornflour made into a paste with a little cold water.

Serve with mashed potato.

Marinated
Chicken Wings

SERVES 1 (MULTIPLY AS NEEDED)

- 3 chicken wings
- 2 tablespoons light soy sauce
- 1 tablespoon fish sauce
- 1 teaspoon sesame oil
- 1 tablespoon honey
- 2 cloves garlic, peeled and finely chopped

Remove the tips from the chicken wings and save for making stock and soup. Marinate the chicken wings in the remaining ingredients for at least 2 hours before putting into a baking dish and baking in the oven at 170°C for 40 minutes. Line the baking tin as the marinade may stick as it cooks. Increase marinade quantity to cover the number of chicken wings you cook.

Potato and Sweetcorn Drumsticks

This recipe can be multiplied easily to feed the number of people you are catering for. Allow 2 chicken drumsticks and 200 g potatoes per person (200 g is approximately 1 medium potato).

SERVES 2

- 1 tablespoon honey
- 1 teaspoon chilli paste (or to taste)
- 2 teaspoons white wine vinegar
- salt and pepper
- 4 chicken drumsticks
- 400 g potatoes, cut into wedges
- 4 French shallots, cut into wedges
- 4 tablespoons vegetable oil
- 2 sprigs rosemary
- 1 tablespoon fresh thyme, finely chopped
- 1–2 cobs corn, kernels removed
- 2 cloves garlic, chopped (optional)
- 1 teaspoon ground cumin (optional)

Mix together the honey, chilli paste, vinegar and season with salt and pepper. Rub this mixture into the chicken drumsticks.

Place the potatoes and shallots into a roasting pan and drizzle with the oil. Lay the chicken drumsticks on top of the potatoes and scatter over the rosemary and thyme. Roast in a 200°C oven for 20 minutes, then baste the chicken with the juices. Stir in the corn that has been removed from the cobs.

Return to the oven and cook a further 30 minutes or until the juices from the chicken are clear.

Note: For extra flavour add 2 cloves peeled chopped garlic and 1 teaspoon ground cumin.

Baked Potatoes

Wash the number of large potatoes required – allowing one per person and a few extra for hungry people. Pierce each potato a few times with a cake tester, wrap in foil and bake in a moderate (180°C) oven for 1½ hours until soft OR roll potatoes in olive oil, place in a baking dish and cook. Carefully cut the tops off the potatoes and then have various toppings on hand for the guests to help themselves.

Suggested toppings include left-over bolognese sauce, chopped ham, grated tasty cheese, sour cream, coleslaw.

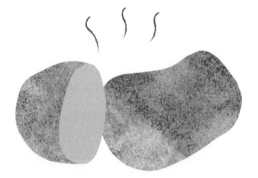

Cheese Puffs

These can be frozen and reheated in the microwave.
Delicious with soup or a casserole. Quick and easy to whip up if you
have unexpected visitors.

MAKES 28 SMALL OR 24 LARGER PUFFS (DOUBLE FOR 50)

- 2 brown onions, peeled and finely chopped
- oil, for frying
- ½ cup (125 ml) milk
- 1 egg, lightly beaten
- 1 teaspoon Dijon mustard
- 2 cups (250 g) grated tasty cheese
- 4 rashers bacon, chopped and cooked (or left-over ham)
- 1 cup (150 g) self-raising flour
- 1 tablespoon finely chopped parsley or chives
- salt and pepper, to taste

Lightly fry chopped onion in a little oil until it is translucent.

Combine the milk, egg and mustard and whisk in a large bowl. Add cheese, bacon, onion, sifted flour, parsley, salt and pepper and mix well.

Line an oven tray with baking paper. Drop dessertspoons of the mixture onto the tray and bake in a hot (200–230°C) oven for approximately 10 minutes.

Vegetable Curry

This recipe can easily be multiplied to serve the number you are catering for.

SERVES 4

- 3 cups vegetables, cut up into bite-sized chunks – cauliflower, broccoli, carrot, sweet potato, potato, zucchini (courgette), beans, pumpkin, or any other vegetable you have on hand
- 2 teaspoons vegetable oil
- 1 medium onion, peeled and chopped
- ½ small red chilli, deseeded and chopped finely or ½ teaspoon dried chilli
- 1 clove garlic, peeled and finely chopped
- 1 teaspoon peeled and grated fresh ginger
- ½ teaspoon ground cumin
- ½ teaspoon turmeric
- ½ teaspoon tomato sauce
- 1½ cups (375 ml) chicken or vegetable stock (can use 1 stock cube or 1 teaspoon stock powder mixed with 375 ml water)

Break cauli and broccoli into florets (if using). Heat oil in a large saucepan, add onion, chilli, garlic, ginger and spices and stir over moderate heat for 1–2 minutes. Add remaining ingredients, mix well, bring to the boil. Cover saucepan and simmer for 15 minutes. Remove the lid and simmer for a further 10 minutes, or until vegetables are tender but still a little crunchy.

Chickpea Pasta

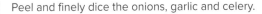

SERVES 24 (DOUBLE TO SERVE 50)

- **6 onions**
- **8 cloves garlic**
- **8 sticks celery**
- **1 cup (250 ml) olive or safflower oil**
- **8 sprigs rosemary**
- **12 x 440 g cans chickpeas**
- **salt and pepper**
- **1.8 kg dried pasta shells**
- **180 g grated parmesan**

Peel and finely dice the onions, garlic and celery.

Add the oil to a large pot on a low heat. Strip the leaves from the stalks of rosemary and add to the pot. Gently fry until crispy. Remove rosemary and leave infused oil behind. To this add the onion, garlic and celery and cook until soft and sweet, stirring occasionally.

Add the chickpeas, including the juice, plus about 15 cans water. Bring to the boil and simmer for 15 minutes. Season well with salt and pepper.

Remove half the chickpea mixture and blend with a stick blender or food processor to a smooth paste. Return this to the pan. Add the pasta to the pot and bring to the boil, then simmer until cooked, adding more water if necessary. Add the majority of the parmesan but reserve some for serving. Check seasoning and ladle into bowls. Sprinkle with remaining parmesan and serve.

Suggestion: Add 1 bag of frozen peas for the last few minutes of cooking to add colour and extra nutrition or, if needing extra liquid, add a can of crushed tomatoes instead.

THRIFTY DESSERT TIPS FOR A CROWD

- When making **hot desserts** for a large number of people, it is easy to multiply the recipe at the time of mixing (e.g. fruit crumble, or a self-saucing pudding), to serve the number of people you are catering for. You will need larger dishes to bake them in, or several if using smaller dishes. If recipe says to bake for 40 minutes, check larger quantity after the 40 minutes to see if dessert is baked. If not, then check every 10 minutes thereafter until cooked through. *Do not increase oven temperature to cook quicker.*

- If making **cold desserts**, it is better to make several batches rather than one large batch. They are all very easy to make and you may choose to make 2 of each, rather than 6 of the one dessert.

Flummery

To serve 50, double the recipe, then make it three times.

SERVES 8

- **1 packet jelly – flavour of your choice**
- **1 can (390 ml) evaporated milk, chilled in the fridge for at least 24 hours**
- **fruit of your choice – e.g. berries with a strawberry or raspberry jelly, fresh mango with an orange or mango jelly**

Make jelly up with 1 cup (250 ml) boiling water and allow to cool but not set.

Whip chilled evaporated milk until thick like whipped cream. Add cooled jelly and whip until mixed. Stir in fruit of your choice and refrigerate.

Lemon Sago

To serve 50, triple the recipe, then make it three times.

SERVES 6

- ⅔ cup (130 g) sago
- ¼ cup (55 g) caster sugar
- 2 tablespoons golden syrup
- 2 cups (500 ml) water
- ⅓ cup (80 ml) lemon juice
- 2 egg whites at room temperature

Boil the sago, sugar and golden syrup in the water and lemon juice until clear, stirring frequently. Pour into a bowl and cool a little.

Beat the 2 egg whites until thick and frothy then gently add to the lemon sago mixture and stir in well.

Mixture is easily doubled or tripled, but if doing this, be careful and keep stirring so that it doesn't catch on the bottom of the pan.

Serve with fruit salad and ice cream or whipped cream, if desired.

Trifle

If serving trifle for 50 people, make separate Swiss rolls and make each trifle quantity individually – don't try to make a giant Swiss roll and a multitude of jellies at once.

SERVES 6

- **1 Swiss roll (jam roll) – can use up a stale one here or any stale left-over sponge or plain cake spread with a little jam (to make your own Swiss roll, see recipe on page 156)**
- **a little sherry or apple juice**
- **1 packet jelly**
- **2 cups (500 ml) boiling water**
- **1 quantity of Creamy Custard (see page 36)**
- **fruit of your choice, to taste**
- **whipped cream, for topping**
- **toasted flaked almonds, for decorating**

Slice the Swiss roll and place decoratively around a glass bowl. Sprinkle on a little sweet sherry or apple juice to moisten the cake. Make up a jelly with the boiling water and set in a shallow tin, such as a lamington pan.

Make custard and cool (cover top of custard with baking paper and press down to stop a skin forming on the top as it cools).

To put the trifle together, cut set jelly into cubes. Pour some cooled custard over the soaked cake, place on some fruit and half the jelly cubes, pour over remaining custard, place on more fruit and the remaining jelly cubes. Decorate the top with whipped cream and toasted flaked almonds.

Suggested combinations: Raspberry or strawberry jelly with berries of any sort and/or drained poached plums OR orange or mango jelly with chopped fresh mango and tinned pineapple – if using this combination, spread the cake with lemon curd instead of jam.

Recipe for Swiss Roll

CUTS INTO 8–10 SLICES

- 3 x 60 g eggs
- ½ cup (115 g) caster sugar, plus extra for sprinkling
- ½ teaspoon pure vanilla essence
- 1 cup (150 g) self-raising flour
- 3 tablespoons hot water
- jam or lemon curd

Beat whole eggs until thick and creamy. Gradually beat in caster sugar and beat again for 5 minutes. Add vanilla essence.

Sift the self-raising flour and gently fold into the egg and sugar mixture with a metal spoon. Add hot water, folding in quickly but gently.

Pour mixture into a greased and lined 30 cm x 20 cm shallow tin. Bake in a moderately hot (180°C) oven for 10–12 minutes.

Turn sponge out onto a sheet of baking paper that has been sprinkled with caster sugar. Roll up from the short end. When cooled a little, carefully unroll and spread over jam or lemon curd, then roll up again.

Variation: Make a chocolate Swiss roll by sifting 1 tablespoon cocoa with the flour. The custard can be made into a chocolate custard by adding 1 tablespoon Nesquik to the custard mixture when cooking. This then becomes a chocolate trifle. Poached apricots or plums are delicious fruits to serve with this variation.

Fruit Crumble

SERVES 50

- **4 kg of either fresh or tinned fruit (apples, pears, peaches, apricots, plums, rhubarb or you may use a combination for larger numbers; if using fresh fruit, cook fruit before topping with the crumble; do not pre-cook fresh berries)**
- **ground cinnamon**

CRUMBLE WITH HONEY
- **6 cups (900 g) plain flour**
- **10 cups (1 kg) rolled oats (not quick oats)**
- **8 teaspoons honey or sugar, to taste**
- **2 cups (500 ml) vegetable oil (not a strong flavoured oil such as olive oil)**
- **3 cups (270 g) desiccated coconut**

Preheat oven to 160°C. Put fruit into a large mixing bowl and add cinnamon. Stir to combine. Divide between baking dishes.

Mix flour, oats, honey (or sugar), oil and coconut all together in the same bowl as you mixed the fruit in.

Spoon the oat mixture over the fruit and smooth down. Bake in the oven for 30 minutes. Serve with a dollop of yoghurt, custard, cream or ice cream.

 Fruits for a baked fruit crumble are interchangeable. Use only one fruit or a combination, such as rhubarb and apple; rhubarb and plum; rhubarb and any berry; apple and strawberry; apricot and blueberry; peach and strawberry or blackberry; quince and apple.

Kaz's Crumble Topping

SERVES 50

- **640 g cold butter, chopped**
- **600 g self-raising flour**
- **320 g almond meal**
- **480 g brown sugar**
- **240 g shredded coconut**
- **160 g slivered almonds**
- **6 kg cooked fruit**

Rub butter into flour and almond meal until mixture forms a crumble (can be done in a large food processor, in batches if necessary).

Tip into a large bowl and mix in brown sugar, shredded coconut and slivered almonds. Mix well and pour over around 6 kg of cooked fruit.

Bake in a moderate (180°C) oven for 30 minutes. Will need to use several large ovenproof dishes for this quantity.

Marguerite Pudding

SERVES 6 (SEE NOTE)

- **60 g butter**
- **60 g caster sugar**
- **1 egg, beaten**
- **125 g self-raising flour**
- **a little milk**
- jam

Beat the butter and sugar until pale and creamy. Add the egg, then the flour and a little milk to make a light batter.

To steam the pudding, place a heatproof saucer upside down in a large saucepan, add water to cover the saucer and bring to the boil.

Line a well-greased pudding steamer with jam, then pour in the pudding mixture. Cover pudding with baking paper, place the lid on and put in the saucepan, on top of the saucer. Turn heat down to low, and gently steam for 1 hour – no longer, or it will spoil. During steaming, check water level to ensure saucepan doesn't boil dry; if you need to add extra water during steaming, use boiling water, not cold water, as this will stop the cooking process. To turn out, carefully lift steamer out of the saucepan, remove lid and baking paper, place a large plate over the steamer and carefully turn upside down. The pudding should slide out of the steamer onto the plate. Serve immediately, with hot custard, cream or ice cream.

Note: This mixture is cooked in a small pudding steamer. Double the recipe and cook in a large pudding steamer to serve 12. To serve 50 make 4 separate double quantities of this recipe. You can precook the puddings, then reheat in the microwave to serve. See flavour alternatives on next page.

Alternatives:

• Make chocolate by leaving out 1 tablespoon flour and adding 1 tablespoon cocoa and 1 teaspoon instant coffee mixed in with the milk to dissolve coffee granules.

• Peel and chop 1 apple and put in bottom of pudding basin, pour over 2 tablespoons maple syrup, then put in pudding mixture and steam.

• Spread 2 tablespoons brown sugar in base of greased pudding basin and add 1 diced banana before putting in pudding mixture and steaming.

• Add 90 g sultanas and 1 tablespoon grated lemon rind to the pudding mixture before steaming.

TIP

For a delicious **toffee-like crust** on a steamed pudding, grease the pudding basin with butter, then shake some brown sugar lightly over the base and sides.

Basic Slab Cake

Slab cakes are very useful when catering for large numbers.
This is the basic recipe but see the flavour variations on next page.

SERVES 25 (MAKE 2 CAKES TO SERVE 50)

- **250 g butter, melted and cooled**
- **4 eggs**
- **2 cups (440 g) caster sugar**
- **1 cup (250 ml) milk**
- **3 cups (450 g) self-raising flour, sifted**
- **1 teaspoon pure vanilla essence**

Beat all ingredients together until smooth – will be quite a runny mixture depending on the brand of flour used. Pour into a 22 cm x 30 cm x 4 cm tin lined with baking paper. Bake in a moderate oven (170°C) for approximately 45 minutes or until a cake tester comes out clean.

VARIATIONS

- **Apple** or **Apricot Cake** Dollop one small tin of pie apple or pie apricot over the top before baking. Dust with icing sugar to serve.

- **Tea Cake** When cake comes out of the oven, brush while hot with melted butter, then sprinkle over the cake a mixture of 2 tablespoons caster sugar and 1 teaspoon cinnamon. When cold, slice and butter as for a tea cake.

- **Marble Cake** Divide mixture into 3 before cooking. Add a little pink colouring to ⅓ then some cocoa to another ⅓. Dollop into the tin, then swirl with a knife to give a marbled effect.

- **Orange Cake** Use ½ cup (125 ml) milk and ½ cup (125 ml) fresh orange juice plus grated rind of 1 orange. Ice with orange icing made using orange juice instead of hot water. This mixture will be too soft to put dried fruit into as the fruit will sink to the bottom.

TIP

Make self-raising flour from plain flour by sifting 1 teaspoon baking powder into 1 cup (150 g) plain flour. Sift well before using to fully distribute the baking powder.

Coconut Jam Slice

SERVES 25 (MAKE 2 CAKES TO SERVE 50)

- **125 g butter**
- **½ cup (115 g) caster sugar**
- **1 egg**
- **1½ cups (225 g) self-raising flour**
- **jam, flavour of your choice**

TOPPING
- **2 eggs, beaten**
- **1 cup (220 g) caster sugar**
- **2 cups (180 g) desiccated coconut**

Line a 25 cm x 30 cm slice tin with baking paper.

Beat the butter with the caster sugar. Add the egg and beat again. Mix in the flour. (Can be done in the food processor.) This pastry is very soft.

Roll pastry out on a pastry sheet, place the lined tin over the rolled-out pastry, then carefully invert. Patch up any pastry holes with spare pastry.

Mix together the topping ingredients in a bowl.

Spread jam over the base, then spoon over the topping. Bake in a 170°C oven for 25 minutes.

Apple Cake

SERVES 25 (MAKE 2 CAKES TO SERVE 50)

- 6 apples, peeled and chopped
- 2 cups (440 g) caster sugar
- 2 cups (280 g) walnuts or pecans (optional)
- 2 teaspoons ground ginger
- 2 teaspoons cinnamon
- 1 teaspoon bicarbonate of soda
- 1 cup (150 g) self-raising flour
- 1 cup (150 g) plain flour
- 4 eggs
- 2 teaspoons pure vanilla essence
- 250 g butter, melted and cooled

Mix all together well and pour into 2 large greased and lined baking tins or 4 small pans. Bake in moderate (180°C) oven 45 minutes. Can be iced or sprinkled with icing sugar or eaten warm, sliced and spread with butter.

WHAT TO DO
WITH THE GLUT

CHUTNEY AND RELISH TIPS

Both chutney and relish are mixtures of vegetables and/or fruit, spiced and flavoured and **cooked in vinegar to do the preserving**.

The general acceptance is that **chutney refers to the sweetened mixtures** where the product is thick and of an even texture, not unlike jam but without the jellied quality. The taste should be mellow. To achieve this, the fruits and vegetables are chopped small and cooked for a long time slowly.

The basic procedures for preparing either chutney or relish are similar. The vegetables should be **ripe but not overripe**. Diseased produce should not be used and damaged areas should be discarded. Fruit should be almost ripe or ripe, depending on the type.

Chutney and relish should be stored at least 6–8 weeks for the flavours to develop and mature. Tasting these products while still warm will give a false idea of flavour, which may seem too spicy and hot, but this will modify on storage.

Remember **it is sugar and vinegar that helps preserve chutneys and relishes**, and salt and vinegar for pickles.

Relishes are thickened with flour/mustard/cornflour etc. whereas chutneys are not thickened artificially, but are reduced by cooking to a thick consistency. Always mix flour and mustard with a little extra vinegar, not water.

It's best to **cover relish in a jar with a lid**, rather than cellophane. This is because, over time, the cellophane covers allow some evaporation, which can dry out the relish and make it shrink in the jar. Don't waste this relish though, use it to flavour curries, casseroles, pasties and sausage rolls.

Delicious Chutney

MAKES APPROXIMATELY 4 X 375 G JARS

- 500 g green apples
- 250 g onions
- 250 g white sugar
- 125 g brown sugar
- 250 g peeled tomatoes
- 30 g chopped celery
- ¼ cup (30 g) chopped green beans
- grated rind of 1 lemon
- 125 g chopped dates
- 250 g sultanas
- 125 g dried cranberries
- 30 g preserved ginger
- 30 g dark plum jam
- 15 g honey
- 15 g salt
- 10 g ground ginger
- pinch pepper
- pinch pimento (allspice)
- 125 ml vinegar

Peel and cut up apples and onions, then place in a pan. Sprinkle with half of the sugar and leave overnight.

Add all remaining ingredients, except the vinegar. Stir while bringing to a simmer. Simmer slowly for 1 hour and then add the vinegar. Boil until the mass is very pulpy.

Bottle when cool.

This recipe was awarded 2nd Prize at the Gippsland Hills 2011 Group Exhibition.

Fruit Chutney

MAKES APPROXIMATELY 8 X 375 G JARS

This recipe was designed to take advantage of the creator's prolific home garden.

- 3 large onions
- 1 kg tomatoes
- 2 large Granny Smith apples
- 3 cups (660 g) raw sugar
- ¾ cup (130 g) sultanas
- ¾ cup (130 g) raisins
- 1 tablespoon whole cloves (in a little muslin bag)
- 1 tablespoon salt
- good pinch cayenne pepper
- good pinch ground ginger
- 5 cups (1.25 litres) brown vinegar

Peel and chop the onions. Remove the skin from the tomatoes and chop them coarsely. Peel, core and dice the apples.

Put all the ingredients into a pan, stir over low heat until the sugar dissolves. Bring to the boil and then simmer uncovered for 2–2½ hours or until thick.

Remove the bag of cloves before turning the chutney into hot sterilised jars and sealing.

Apple, Mint and Raisin Chutney

MAKES APPROXIMATELY 4 X 375 G JARS

- **450 g cooking apples,** peeled and chopped
- **125 g raisins, chopped**
- **¾ cup (35 g) chopped mint**
- **1½ cups (375 ml) white vinegar**
- **1 cup (220 g) raw sugar**
- **1 teaspoon mustard powder**
- **3 onions, peeled and finely chopped**
- **1 teaspoon chilli powder**
- **1 teaspoon salt**

Combine all ingredients in a saucepan, stir over a low heat until the sugar has dissolved. Increase the heat, bring back to the boil, then reduce heat and boil gently for approximately 1 hour or until the mixture has thickened.

Remove from the heat. Pour mixture into sterilised jars, seal and label.

TIP

Don't forget that **windfall fruit** may still be usable. Just cut off any bruised bits, don't throw all the fruit out.

Basic Sweet Muffins

MAKES 12

- **2 heaped cups (320 g) self-raising flour**
- **⅓ cup (80 g) caster sugar**
- **2 cored, peeled and chopped apples**
- **½ teaspoon cinnamon**
- **½ cup (125 ml) grapeseed oil**
- **1 egg**
- **1 cup (250 ml) milk**

Mix flour and sugar together with apples and cinnamon. In a separate bowl mix the remaining ingredients. Gently mix both together. Do not overmix or muffins will be tough.

Place spoonfuls into a greased muffin tin. Bake in moderate (180°C) oven for 20 minutes.

Variation: Instead of the apples and cinnamon, add these alternative flavours to the dry ingredients before mixing with the remaining ingredients:

- ½ cup (90 g) choc chips and grated rind of ½ orange
- 1 cup (160 g) chopped dates
- 1 cup (155 g) blueberries

Streusel Topping for Muffins

- 1 tablespoon brown sugar
- 1 tablespoon plain flour
- 1 teaspoon cinnamon
- 1 tablespoon butter
- 2 tablespoons chopped walnuts (optional)

Rub the ingredients together with your fingertips to make a crumble mixture. Place small spoonfuls on top of muffins before baking.

TIP

Grated or diced **apples or pears** make tasty additions to a basic muffin or cake recipe.

If you have a **dehydrator** you can dehydrate plums, apricots, peaches, pears and apples.

Apricot Chutney

The choice of vinegar and the spice line up can be changed to suit your taste.

MAKES APPROXIMATELY 6 X 375 G JARS

- **1 kg ripe apricots**
- **2 large Granny Smith apples**
- **1 large onion**
- **375 g sultanas**
- **225 g brown sugar**
- **2 teaspoons dry mustard**
- **2 teaspoons salt**
- **2 teaspoons ground ginger**
- **2 teaspoons cinnamon**
- **½ teaspoon cayenne pepper**
- **2 cups (500 ml) white vinegar**

Stone and chop apricots. Peel and chop the apples. Chop the onion.

Put all the ingredients into a large saucepan, preferably enamel. Bring slowly to a simmer and simmer for 2 hours, stirring as needed until thick.

Spoon into hot sterilised jars, cool and seal.

Tomato Apricot Chutney

MAKES ABOUT 5 X 375 G JARS

- **250 g dried apricots**
- **2 cups (500 ml) water**
- **2 teaspoons oil**
- **2 teaspoons yellow mustard seeds**
- **2 teaspoons cumin seeds**
- **8 large tomatoes, peeled and chopped**
- **4 medium onions, finely chopped**
- **1 cup (250 ml) orange juice**
- **⅓ cup (80 ml) lemon juice**
- **⅓ cup (90 g) tomato paste**
- **2 cups (500 ml) white vinegar**
- **2 cups (440 g) sugar**
- **1 tablespoon soy sauce**
- **1 tablespoon grated fresh ginger**
- **1 teaspoon salt, or to taste**

Combine apricots and water in a saucepan. Bring to the boil and boil for 5 minutes.

Heat the oil in a frying pan, add the mustard and cumin seeds. Cook, stirring for 4 minutes then cool. Crush the seeds with a rolling pin.

Combine seeds with the undrained apricot mixture and the tomatoes in a large heavy-based pan. Add all the remaining ingredients and place over medium heat, stirring constantly until the sugar is dissolved. Bring to the boil, reduce heat and simmer uncovered for 1 hour.

Pour into hot sterilised jars and seal when cold.

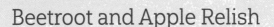

Beetroot and Apple Relish

MAKES APPROXIMATELY 4 X 375 G JARS

- ½ tablespoon oil
- ½ diced red onion
- 400 g grated beetroot
- 175 g grated green apple
- ½ cup (125 ml) white wine vinegar
- ½ cup (125 ml) balsamic vinegar
- ½ cup (110 g) brown sugar
- 1 tablespoon lemon juice
- ½ teaspoon Dijon mustard

Heat the oil in a large saucepan and sauté the onion until transparent. Add all the ingredients and cook on the lowest heat for 2 hours, until it resembles jam.

Cool before bottling.

7 Minute Raspberry Jam

MAKES APPROXIMATELY 5 X 375 G JARS

- **1 kg raspberries**
- **750 g sugar**
- **juice 1 lemon**

Bring raspberries to the boil, add sugar and lemon juice, stir until sugar dissolves, then boil for 7 minutes. Pour into sterilised jars.

JAM EXTENDER

If you wish to **extend the number of jars of jam** from the raspberries or blackberries you have cooked, add a little cooked apple pulp. The apple will take on the flavour of the raspberries or blackberries.

Capsicum and Tomato Relish

As well as being good with cold meats, this recipe makes a delicious sandwich spread. Cornflour makes a clearer and brighter relish and is gluten free.

MAKES APPROXIMATELY 8 X 375 G JARS

- **4 large red capsicums (peppers), seeded**
- **500 g tomatoes, peeled**
- **4 medium onions**
- **2 tablespoons salt**
- **2 cups (500 ml) white vinegar**
- **1½ cups (330 g) sugar**
- **1 tablespoon mustard seeds**
- **2 tablespoons flour or gluten-free cornflour**
- **¼ teaspoon paprika**
- **¼ teaspoon turmeric**
- **½ cup (125 ml) water**

Chop seeded capsicums finely. Chop peeled tomatoes finely. Peel onions and chop finely.

Combine vegetables in a large bowl and sprinkle with salt. Let stand for a few hours or overnight then drain.

In a large saucepan combine vinegar, sugar and mustard seeds. Stir over low heat until sugar dissolves then bring to the boil. Add the vegetables and return to the boil. Boil for 10 minutes.

Combine the flour (or cornflour), paprika and turmeric and mix to a smooth paste with the water, add to the mixture and stir until boiling. Reduce heat and simmer for 10 minutes.

Pour into hot sterilised jars and seal.

Piccalilli

MAKES APPROXIMATELY 8 X 375 G JARS

- 500 g cauliflower, chopped
- 2 carrots, sliced
- 2 celery sticks, sliced
- 2 green tomatoes, chopped
- 1 cucumber, sliced
- 250 g pickling onions, quartered
- 1 cup (100 g) cooking salt
- 5 cups (1.25 litres) white vinegar, plus extra ¼ cup (60 ml)
- 1 cup (220 g) sugar
- 1 tablespoon turmeric
- 1 tablespoon dry mustard
- ¼ teaspoon ground ginger
- 2 cloves garlic, crushed
- 2 small fresh red chillies, chopped
- ¼ cup (30 g) cornflour

Combine cauliflower, carrots, celery, tomatoes, cucumber, onions and salt in large bowl, cover, stand overnight.

Rinse vegetables well under cold water; drain well.

Combine vinegar, sugar, turmeric, mustard, ginger, garlic and chillies in large saucepan. Bring to the boil, add vegetables, simmer, covered, for about 5 minutes or until vegetables are just tender. Stir in blended cornflour and extra vinegar, stir until mixture boils and thickens.

Pour into hot sterilised jars and seal.

Mustard Pickles

MAKES APPROXIMATELY 8 X 375 G JARS

- 1 kg cauliflower florets
- 450 g white onions, sliced
- salt
- 1 cucumber
- 500 ml white distilled vinegar
- 400 g white sugar
- 1 teaspoon capers, rinsed
- 1 small red chilli, chopped
- 3 tablespoons cornflour
- 4 teaspoons dry mustard
- 2 teaspoons turmeric
- ½ teaspoon curry powder
- ½ teaspoon ground ginger

Place the cauliflower florets and onion into a bowl and sprinkle with 3 tablespoons salt. Add cold water to cover and leave overnight, tossing once or twice.

Cut the unpeeled cucumber in half lengthwise, scoop out and discard the seeds. Cut the cucumber into 1 cm dice and toss with 1 tablespoon salt. Leave 30 minutes, then rinse well and drain, gently squeezing out excess water.

Drain the cauliflower and onion.

In a large pot bring the vinegar and sugar to the boil, stirring to dissolve the sugar. Add the cauliflower, onion, cucumber, capers and chilli and bring to the boil.

Mix the cornflour, spices, 1 teaspoon salt and a little cold water to make a paste. Gradually add to the vegetable mixture, stirring constantly, until the mixture boils and thickens. Reduce the heat and simmer for 5 minutes.

Pour into warm sterilised jars and seal. Leave for up to 6 weeks if you can.

This recipe has won First prize at many Polwarth Group Exhibitions.

CHILLIES

TIP

Chop **chillies** in the food processor (with the seeds if you like extra heat) with a good pinch of salt, add juice of ½ lemon and a whole head of garlic peeled. Whizz and mix well in the food processor. Put into sterilised jars and store in the fridge. Will keep nearly 1 year.

Crabapple and carrot relish

MAKES APPROXIMATELY 6 X 375 G JARS

- **1.5 kg crabapples**
- **500 g carrots**
- **2 brown onions**
- **2 large cloves garlic**
- **2 oranges**
- **1 lime, sliced, rind included**
- **350 g sugar**
- **700 ml white vinegar**
- **3 teaspoons salt**
- **1½ tablespoons chopped fresh mint**
- **1 tablespoon cornflour mixed with 3 tablespoons white vinegar**

Peel and core the crabapples. Peel and grate the carrots. Peel and dice the onions and garlic. Chop the oranges into pieces.

Soak the slices of lime in a small quantity of water for 6 hours.

Drain the lime rind then place all the ingredients, except cornflour mixture, into a large pan and cook until soft.

Mix the cornflour with the white vinegar to make a soft slurry. Mix into the relish and boil to thicken.

Bottle, seal and label.

Cucumber Pickles

THIS RECIPE MAKES ABOUT 8 X 375 G JARS

- 2 kg cucumbers
- 1 kg onions
- 1 kg green apples
- 600 ml vinegar, plus a little extra
- 2 tablespoons salt
- 1 dessertspoon curry powder
- 1 level tablespoon turmeric
- 1 tablespoon dry mustard
- 2 tablespoons flour
- 1 kg sugar

Peel and cut up the cucumbers, onions and apples. Boil with the vinegar for ¾ hour.

Mix the dry ingredients, except the sugar, with a little vinegar. Add the paste with the sugar. Bring to the boil and boil until it thickens. Bottle while hot.

PICKLES

Lemon Drops

MAKES ABOUT 36

- **½ cup (125 g) butter**
- **¾ cup (170 g) caster sugar**
- **4 tablespoons lemon zest**
- **½ teaspoon bicarbonate of soda**
- **1 egg**
- **½ cup (125 g) sour cream**
- **⅓ cup (80 ml) lemon juice**
- **2 cups (300 g) plain flour**
- **raw sugar and candied peel, to decorate (optional)**

LEMON GLAZE
- **1 cup (125 g) icing sugar**
- **4–5 teaspoons lemon juice**

Cream butter and sugar, and then add the lemon zest and bicarb soda. Beat in the egg, sour cream and lemon juice, stir until combined. Add the flour.

Place spoonfuls of mixture onto a tray, allowing room for spreading, and bake in a moderate (180°C) oven for 8–10 minutes.

Meanwhile, make the lemon glaze by whisking the icing sugar and lemon juice together in a bowl.

Transfer the cooked biscuits to a wire rack and, while they are still warm, brush with lemon glaze. If desired, sprinkle with raw sugar and candied peel.

Note: Limes could be substituted for the lemons.

Lemon Marmalade

MAKES APPROXIMATELY 4 X 375 G JARS

- 1 kg thin-skinned lemons
- 1.25 litres boiling water
- 1.6 kg sugar

Halve the lemons lengthwise and slice very thinly – aim to have the slices 2 mm wide or less. Remove all seeds.

Place the lemon slices in a large heatproof bowl and pour over the boiling water. Stand for 24 hours.

Pour the contents of the bowl into a large saucepan and bring to the boil, reduce the heat and cook for 1 hour without the lid on the pan.

Add the sugar and gently bring back to the boil, stirring as the sugar dissolves – again don't place the lid on the pot.

Boil for 30 minutes, carefully and occasionally stirring. Remove any scum if it appears on the surface of the marmalade.

Pour into hot sterilised jars.

Lemon-flavoured Butter

Combine rind and juice of 1 lemon with 100 g butter. Mix well, then pat butter into a roll shape. Wrap in plastic wrap. Slice and use on grilled fish, or wrap fillets of fish in foil with a slice of the lemon butter, some finely chopped parsley and season with white pepper. Bake until fish is cooked. This lemon butter can be frozen in ice cubes until needed.

Mint Lemon Drink

MAKES ABOUT 1 LITRE

- 4 cups (1 litre) water
- 2 cups (440 g) sugar
- 1 cup (20 g) crushed mint
- a little finely cut lemon peel
- strained juice of 6 lemons
- lemon slices and mint sprigs, to garnish

Boil the water and sugar. Pour the mixture over the crushed mint in a jug, and add a little finely cut lemon peel. Add the lemon juice. Chill and serve with slices of lemon and mint sprigs.

Lemon Cordial

MAKES ABOUT 1 LITRE

- juice 6 large lemons, strained
- 4 cups (880 g) sugar
- grated rind 3 lemons
- 1 tablespoon citric acid
- 2 teaspoons Epsom salts
- 900 ml boiling water

Place all ingredients in a saucepan. Stir over a low heat until sugar has dissolved. When cool, bottle and store in the refrigerator. Dilute with water for drinking.

Melon Pickles

This has been favourably commented upon in the Branch entry at the local Show. This recipe was used when tomatoes and other vegetables were not readily available in the 1940s.

MAKES APPROXIMATELY 10 X 375 G JARS

- **2 kg jam melon (citron melon)**
- **1 kg onions**
- **3 cups (660 g) sugar**
- **½ teaspoon salt**
- **1.5 litres white vinegar, plus a little extra**
- **1 dessertspoon whole peppercorns**
- **1 dessertspoon whole allspice**
- **1 dessertspoon whole cloves**
- **3 tablespoons cornflour**
- **1 tablespoon dry mustard**
- **1 tablespoon turmeric**
- **1 tablespoon curry powder**

Cut the melon into small pieces and dice the onions.

In a pot add the sugar, salt and vinegar to the melon and onion.

Tie the whole spices in a piece of cloth (muslin) and add to the melon and onion. Bring to the boil and cook for 1–1 ½ hours until soft.

Blend the cornflour and remaining spices with a little vinegar and add to the pot. Cook a further ¾ hour until thick, stirring often.

Bottle while hot.

Nectarine Jam

MAKES APPROXIMATELY 6 X 375 G JARS

- 1 kg ripe nectarines
- 1 kg white granulated sugar
- freshly squeezed juice of 2 lemons

Cut the nectarines into 1 cm cubes. In a china bowl layer nectarines and sugar until all fruit and sugar have been used. Pour over lemon juice, cover with a cloth and leave overnight.

Reserving the liquid, drain the fruit and set aside. Scrape all liquid and any undissolved sugar into a heavy based saucepan or preserving pan. Boil rapidly for 5 minutes, add fruit and cook for a further 5 minutes. Cook at a full rolling boil until setting point is reached.

Pot into sterilised jars, seal and label when cool.

Spiced Peaches

SERVES 6

- 6 peaches
- 2 tablespoons honey
- 500 g plain yoghurt
- 2 tablespoons demerara sugar

SPICED SYRUP
- 4 cups (1 litre) water
- 1 cup (220 g) sugar
- ½ teaspoon mixed spice or cinnamon
- zest and juice of 1 lemon

Mix together syrup ingredients.

Peel, halve (or slice) peaches. Poach peaches in the spiced syrup mixture.

Beat together the honey and yoghurt. Place in a serving dish. Sprinkle with demerara sugar and chill for 2 hours. To serve, place poached peaches in a bowl and serve with the chilled honey yoghurt.

Mustard Pears

MAKES APPROXIMATELY 6 LARGE WIDE-MOUTHED JARS

- 18 Williams pears
- 5 cups (1.25 litres) vinegar, plus a little extra
- 2 cups (440 g) sugar
- 1 tablespoon salt
- 1 large tablespoon turmeric
- 3 tablespoons mustard powder
- 1 large tablespoon curry powder
- 1½–2 tablespoons cornflour

Seed but do not peel the pears, then cut into chunks. The pears should be firm for this recipe, just turning yellow.

Heat vinegar to boiling point with the sugar and salt.

Mix the spices with the cornflour and a little extra vinegar to make a paste, then add to the hot vinegar, stirring well. Boil 2 minutes and then add the pears, simmer for 20 minutes and keep stirring.

Place in jars and seal.

Pears in Wine

MAKES APPROXIMATELY 10 LARGE WIDE-MOUTHED JARS

- 5 kg pears
- 375 ml port wine
- 375 ml vinegar
- 2.5 kg sugar
- 60 g whole cloves

Peel and quarter pears. Put port wine,
vinegar, sugar and cloves in a pan.
Dissolve sugar whilst bringing to the boil.
Add pears and slow boil until pink. Store
in screw top jars.

Pear, Apple and Tomato Chutney

MAKES APPROXIMATELY 8 X 375 G JARS

- 750 g ripe tomatoes
- 450 g brown onions
- 1.25 kg cooking apples
- 500 g firm pears
- 6 garlic cloves
- 100 g fresh ginger
- 1–2 red chillies
- 400 g raisins
- 1 tablespoon salt
- 900 ml white wine vinegar
- 750 g demerara sugar

Skin the tomatoes by cutting a cross in the base of each one, then immerse for a couple of minutes in boiling water. When the skin begins to come away, drain the tomatoes, then peel and chop them.

Chop the onions. Peel, core and chop the apples and pears. Peel and crush the garlic, and peel and grate the fresh ginger. Deseed the red chillies if you want a milder flavour, then chop finely.

Place all the ingredients in a preserving pan, and bring slowly to the boil, stirring until the sugar has dissolved. Once the sugar has dissolved, increase the heat to medium and simmer approximately 1½ hours until the chutney is thick.

Pour into sterilised jars, seal and label.

Pear, Raisin and Ginger Chutney

MAKES APPROXIMATELY 6 X 375 G JARS

- 1.5 kg pears
- 2 brown onions
- 5 cloves garlic
- 5 cm piece of fresh ginger
- 250 g raisins
- 10 whole cloves
- 1–2 red chillies, finely chopped
- 1 litre apple cider vinegar or white vinegar
- 600 g raw sugar

Peel and chop the pears. Peel and dice the onions. Peel and either finely chop or crush the garlic. Peel and grate the fresh ginger.

Place pears, onions, raisins, garlic and ginger into a large pan. Add cloves and finely chopped chillies (remove seeds if you prefer less heat). Add vinegar and cook down a little over low heat, then add sugar. Keep on a low heat until the sugar has dissolved. Bring to the boil and allow to bubble for 30–40 minutes or until thick, stirring frequently to avoid the chutney catching.

When cooked, remove from heat, allow to cool slightly, then bottle in clean, sterilised jars. Seal and label.

Pear and Ginger Paste

MAKES APPROXIMATELY 500 G

- **1 kg pears, peeled and cored**
- **3 cm piece of fresh ginger, peeled and grated**
- **2 teaspoons ground ginger**
- **juice of 2 lemons**
- **750 ml water**
- **750 g sugar**
- **sprig of rosemary (optional)**

Place pears, fresh ginger, ground ginger, lemon juice and water in a large deep pan and cook until pears are tender.

Remove pears carefully from the cooking water. Drain pears, discard cooking liquid and return pears to pan. Break pears up with a potato masher. Add sugar, stirring constantly until mixture thickens to a firm paste. This takes a fair while. Be careful as the mixture spits and catches on the base of the pan if not stirred constantly.

Note: For additional flavour add a sprig of rosemary while cooking the pears, but remove before adding the sugar.

Spicy Pickled Pears or Quinces

MAKES APPROXIMATELY 4 LARGE WIDE-MOUTHED JARS

- 300 g sugar
- 500 ml water
- 1 litre white wine vinegar
- 1 x 8 cm strip of lemon rind
- 1 cinnamon stick
- 6 whole cloves
- 6 whole black peppercorns
- 6 whole allspice
- 8 pears or quinces, peeled, cored and chopped into 2 cm dice

Dissolve sugar, water and vinegar together in a large pan. Add lemon rind, cinnamon stick, whole cloves, whole peppercorns and whole allspice and bring to the boil. Simmer for 10 minutes.

Add prepared pears (or quinces) and cook till they are soft but not mushy – approximately 2½ hours for quinces but only 10–15 minutes for pears.

When fruit is cooked, place into sterilised jars and seal well. Leave aside for about a month before using. This will keep for years if kept in a cool place.

Baked Autumn Fruits

Use a combination of any of the autumn fruits you have on hand or those listed below. This is a very good way to use up fruit if you only have 1 or 2 each of several varieties in the fruit bowl. You won't need all the varieties listed below; you're just looking for a total weight of around 2 kilograms.

SERVES 6

- butter, for greasing
- 2 medium apples
- 2 medium pears
- 600 g large blood plums
- 2 medium peaches
- 400 g fresh or frozen raspberries or 400 g blackberries
- 6 rhubarb stalks
- 125 g brown sugar
- 2 cinnamon sticks or a sprinkling of cinnamon if you don't have cinnamon sticks

Lightly grease a large baking dish with butter. Peel and core the apples and pears. Cut the plums in half and take out the stone. Cut fruit into quarters or eighths if very large.

Arrange the fruits around the baking dish. Sprinkle the brown sugar over the fruit, add the cinnamon, cover with foil and bake for 1 hour at 180°C. Remove from the oven, remove the foil, return to the oven and bake a further 10 minutes uncovered.

Plum, Lime and Coriander Chutney

This chutney is good with cheese, pork chops or roast pork.

MAKES APPROXIMATELY 6 X 375 G JARS

- **1 x 15 cm cinnamon stick**
- **2 tablespoons coriander seeds**
- **1 teaspoon black peppercorns**
- **1–2 star anise**
- **2 kg ripe plums (see note)**
- **2 large brown onions**
- **5–6 cloves garlic**
- **5 cm piece of fresh ginger**
- **500 ml red wine vinegar**
- **2 red chillies (deseed for a milder flavour)**
- **zest and juice of 2 limes**
- **zest and juice of 1 lemon**
- **500 g demerara sugar**

Using a spice mill or mortar and pestle, grind the cinnamon, coriander, peppercorns and star anise until you have a fine powder.

Halve and stone the plums, then roughly chop. Peel and finely chop the onions, then peel and finely chop the garlic and ginger.

Place all the ingredients into a large saucepan and bring slowly to the boil, stirring until the sugar has dissolved. Then increase the heat to medium and simmer gently for approximately 50–60 minutes, stirring often until the chutney is thick. Watch near the end of cooking to make sure that you stir often so that it doesn't catch and burn.

Once the chutney has reduced and thickened, turn off the heat and allow to cool for 10 minutes before placing into hot sterilised jars. Seal and label. Don't open the chutney for one month before using to allow the flavours to develop and mature.

Note: A richer colour is achieved if you use red plums.

Plum or Apricot Sauce

MAKES APPROXIMATELY 3 X 600 ML BOTTLES

- 2 kg ripe plums or apricots
- 250 ml light soy sauce
- 750 g brown onions, peeled and chopped
- cloves from 1–1½ full heads of garlic, peeled and chopped
- 20 cm piece fresh ginger, peeled and chopped
- 1 litre rice wine vinegar
- 1 teaspoon chilli paste
- 2 green chillies, deseeded and chopped
- 1 kg raw sugar (or half raw sugar and half palm sugar)
- 6 star anise, finely ground
- 1 teaspoon black peppercorns, finely ground
- 10 allspice berries, finely ground
- 1 teaspoon coriander seeds, finely ground

Cut plums (or apricots) in half and remove stones.

Put remaining ingredients, except sugar and ground spices, in a large pan. Bring to the boil, cover and simmer for 20 minutes or until ingredients are very soft.

Pass mixture through a mouli or use a stick blender, and then return to the pan. Add sugar and ground spices, and bring back to the boil, stirring frequently to ensure that the sugar dissolves. Simmer the mixture for approximately 40 minutes or until the sauce is thick and creamy.

Pour the sauce into sterilised bottles and seal and label.

Plum and Chilli Jam

MAKES APPROXIMATELY 6 X 250 ML JARS

- 1 kg ripe blood plums
- 750 g sugar
- 1 star anise
- 8 whole cloves
- 2 finely chopped red chillies
- ½ cup (125 ml) red wine vinegar
- 2 teaspoons salt
- ½ teaspoon ground black pepper
- 25 g Jamsetta if the plums are very ripe and therefore lacking in pectin

Finely chop the plums, add to a large pot with all other ingredients (except Jamsetta). Bring to the boil, stirring constantly to warm and melt the sugar. Boil for 25 minutes.

If jam is not setting at this point, add the Jamsetta and boil for another 10 minutes.

Place into warm sterilised jars and seal.

Pumpkin Sauce

Can be used as you use tomato sauce.

MAKES APPROXIMATELY 2 X 600 ML BOTTLES

- 1 teaspoon black peppercorns
- 1 teaspoon whole cloves
- 6 allspice berries
- 2 teaspoons ground nutmeg
- 1 teaspoon ground ginger
- 2 teaspoons salt
- 1 large brown onion
- 6 cloves garlic
- 1½ cups (375 ml) white vinegar
- 3 cups (750 ml) water
- 1.25 kg pumpkin, peeled and chopped
- ½ cup (110 g) sugar

Grind the whole spices to a fine powder and mix together with the other spices and salt.

Place peeled chopped onions, peeled chopped garlic, and half the vinegar and half the water into a saucepan and cook until soft.

Meanwhile, in a large pan, cook down the pumpkin pieces with the remaining water. When onions are softened add to the pumpkin along with the blended spices. Cook for 5 minutes then add sugar and remaining vinegar.

Process or blend with a stick blender until smooth. Continue cooking until desired sauce consistency is reached.

Cool 5 minutes then bottle, seal and label.

Pumpkin Soup

SERVES 4

- 30 g butter
- 1 onion, chopped
- 1 tablespoon flour
- 2½ cups (625 ml) chicken stock
- 1 kg pumpkin, cooked and mashed
- 1 teaspoon brown sugar
- ¼ teaspoon curry powder
- ¼ teaspoon nutmeg
- salt and pepper, to taste
- 1 cup (250 ml) milk (or ¾ cup/185 ml milk and ¼ cup/60 ml pouring cream)
- dollop of thick cream, to serve
- chopped chives

Melt the butter and cook onion until soft. Blend in the flour and cook until bubbly. Remove from heat and stir in stock. Stir over heat until boiled and thickened. Add mashed pumpkin, sugar, curry powder, nutmeg, salt and pepper. Add milk and heat without boiling.

When serving add a dollop of cream and sprinkle with chives or parsley.

Pumpkin Scones

MAKES APPROXIMATELY 12 SCONES

- 30 g butter
- 1 tablespoon sugar
- 1 teaspoon grated lemon rind
- 1 cup (250 g) cold mashed pumpkin
- 1 egg, beaten
- ⅓ cup (80 ml) milk
- 2 cups (300 g) self-raising flour
- ½ teaspoon salt
- 1 teaspoon nutmeg

Cream butter and sugar, add lemon and pumpkin,
then beaten egg and milk. Add flour, salt and nutmeg.
Knead lightly, cut with floured scone cutter. Bake for
12–15 minutes in hot oven (200°C).

Pumpkin Fruit Cake

MAKES 1 X 20 CM CAKE

- 500 g mixed fruits
- 2 tablespoons brandy, sherry or rum
- 125 g butter
- ¾ cup (170 g) caster sugar
- 2 eggs
- 2 dessertspoons golden syrup
- 1 cup (250 g) cooked cold mashed pumpkin
- 2 cups (300 g) self-raising flour

Chop the fruit, sprinkle with the brandy, and stand overnight (or several hours).

Cream butter and sugar and add the well beaten eggs. Add golden syrup and pumpkin. Mix well, then add the fruit and sifted flour.

Place in a lined 15 cm cake tin and bake in a slow (150°C) oven about 45 minutes–1 hour. Test and, if not cooked through, continue cooking for another 15 minutes then re-test.

Note: It's important to cook fruit cakes slowly at a low temperature.

TOMATO TIPS

- When **dehydrating tomatoes**, first slice them vertically as they will stay firmer than if sliced horizontally, then sprinkle the tomato slices with salt.

- For **long term storage** and once the tomatoes have been dehydrated, dip the slices in white vinegar and store in a dark dry cupboard in sterilised jars covered with olive oil.

- Always store tomatoes at **room temperature** for maximum flavour.

- To stop a jar of **tomato paste** going mouldy, cover the surface of the paste with olive oil. Replace the lid and store in fridge until you need it again.

Green Tomato and Cauliflower Pickles

MAKES APPROXIMATELY 10 X 375 G JARS

- **3 kg green tomatoes**
- **750 g brown onions**
- **1 small cauliflower**
- **¼ cup (25 g) salt**
- **375 ml malt vinegar, plus a little extra**
- **750 g sugar**
- **¼ cup (35 g) plain flour**
- **2 teaspoons curry powder**
- **2 teaspoons turmeric**
- **½ tablespoon dry mustard**
- **¼ teaspoon cayenne pepper**
- **1 teaspoon ground cloves**

Slice the tomatoes, dice the onions, cut the cauliflower into florets.

Place the vegetables in a stainless steel container, sprinkle the salt over vegetables and leave to stand overnight, or at least 10 hours.

In a large saucepan combine the vinegar and sugar and bring to the boil, stirring to dissolve sugar. Add the drained, soaked vegetables and cook over a moderate heat for 20 minutes or until the onion is soft and translucent, stirring occasionally.

Combine the flour and spices with a little extra malt vinegar.

Remove the vegetable mixture from the heat and thoroughly combine with the flour mixture. Return to heat and cook, stirring continuously, for a few minutes until the mixture thickens and there is no 'floury' taste. Be careful that it does not stick.

Bottle while hot and cover with a jam seal moistened with vinegar.

Fruit Chutney

MAKES APPROXIMATELY 8 X 375 G JARS

- 1 kg tomatoes
- 3 large onions
- 2 large Granny Smith apples
- 3 cups (660 g) raw sugar
- 90 g sultanas
- 90 g raisins
- 1 tablespoon whole cloves (in a little muslin bag)
- 1 tablespoon salt
- good pinch cayenne pepper
- good pinch ground ginger
- 5 cups (1.25 litres) brown vinegar

Remove the skin from the tomatoes and chop them coarsely. Peel and chop the onions. Peel, core and dice the apples.

Put all the ingredients into a pan, stir over low heat until the sugar dissolves. Bring to the boil and then simmer uncovered for 2–2½ hours or until thick.

Baked Stuffed Tomatoes

Remove stalk end from tomato and scoop out centre. Fill each tomato with breadcrumbs seasoned with pepper and salt, a little finely chopped onion, or any seasoning liked, and a little of the tomato centre. Dot with butter and bake about 20–25 minutes at 180°C.

Tomato Pie

Skin tomatoes by dropping into boiling water. Remove at once when skin will come away. Cut in thick slices. Butter pie dish and put in a layer of tomatoes, sprinkle with pepper and salt, then a layer of white breadcrumbs. Continue until dish is full with breadcrumbs on top. Dot with butter and bake 20–30 minutes. For a variation onion may be added to mixture.

Tomato Sauce

MAKES APPROXIMATELY 8 X 600 ML BOTTLES

- 7 kg ripe tomatoes
- 1 kg onions
- 1 kg apples
- 60 g garlic (optional)
- 30 g ground ginger
- pinch cayenne pepper
- 30 g cloves
- 30 g allspice
- 5 cups (1.25 litres) white vinegar
- 180 g salt
- 1 kg sugar

Cut up tomatoes, onions, apples and garlic. Add ginger and cayenne. Put ingredients in a saucepan.

Put cloves and allspice in muslin bag and add to tomatoes. Add vinegar and boil 3 hours.

Strain through a sieve. Put back on stove, add salt and sugar and boil for 30 minutes. Strain again, bottle and seal.

· **Tomato Passata**

Chop 10 kg very ripe tomatoes. (It doesn't matter what variety they are.) Place in a stockpot. Add 2 chopped brown onions, salt and white pepper to taste, up to 1 cup (220 g) white sugar (depending on how acidic your tomatoes taste), and 1 cup (250 ml) olive oil. Cook until tomatoes and onions are very soft. Use a stick blender to puree the passata. Fill large sterilised jars, screw on sterilised lids and turn jars upside down for 1 hour and then turn up the right way and the jars will have sealed. Use in casseroles, pasta dishes and soups throughout the year.

Simple Tomato Soup

SERVES 4–6

- 1.5 kg tomatoes, cut in half (see note)
- 2 onions, chopped
- 2 large potatoes, chopped
- 1 tablespoon butter
- 1 tablespoon oil
- 3 litres water
- 1 stock cube
- salt (optional)

Place the tomatoes on a baking tray in a 160°C oven until starting to change colour and break down.

Meanwhile in a large pan place the onion, potato, butter and oil and sauté until soft. Then add the tomatoes, water and stock cube and cook until soft. Salt may be added if desired.

Cool slightly then blend until smooth.

Note: It is not necessary to remove skins or seeds of the tomatoes.

Spicy Tomato Chutney

MAKES APPROXIMATELY 6 X 375 G JARS

- 1 kg ripe tomatoes, peeled and chopped
- 2 large apples, peeled and chopped
- 1 cup (230 g) brown sugar
- 2 brown onions, peeled and chopped
- 1½ cups (375 ml) brown vinegar
- ½ teaspoon chilli powder
- ½ teaspoon dry mustard
- 90 g sultanas
- 1 clove garlic, peeled and crushed
- 2 teaspoons curry powder
- 2 teaspoons ground allspice

Combine all the ingredients in a large saucepan, stir over the heat without boiling until the sugar has dissolved. Increase heat to bring to the boil, then reduce to a gentle simmer and cook uncovered for approximately 1 hour, stirring occasionally, or until the mixture is thick.

Pour into hot sterilised jars, seal and label.

Green Tomato Chutney

MAKES APPROXIMATELY 8 X 375 G JARS

- 2 kg green tomatoes, cored and sliced
- 750 g brown onions, peeled and chopped
- 500 g cooking apples, peeled and chopped
- 600 ml apple cider vinegar
- 4–6 red chillies or to taste
- 6 cloves garlic, peeled
- 30 g fresh ginger, peeled
- 225 g sultanas or raisins
- 500 g raw sugar
- 2 teaspoons salt

Place tomatoes, onions, apples and vinegar in a large pan. Simmer for approximately 30 minutes or until apples and vegetables are soft.

Meanwhile prepare the chillies by removing the membrane (and seeds if wishing for a milder flavour). Transfer to a food processor along with the garlic and ginger and blitz until they form a paste. Add this paste to the pan with the sultanas, sugar and salt. Simmer over a low heat for 5 minutes, stirring until the sugar dissolves. Increase the heat to medium, and continue to simmer for approximately 30 minutes or until thick.

Pour into sterilised jars, seal and label.

Chinese Pickles

This recipe can be halved successfully.

MAKES APPROXIMATELY 12 X 375 G JARS

- 2.5 kg green tomatoes
- 1.5 kg white onions
- 1 bunch celery
- 1 cauliflower
- 500 g green beans
- 2 cucumbers
- 500 g salt
- 2 cups (300 g) plain flour
- 2 tablespoons dry mustard
- 1 tablespoon turmeric
- 1 teaspoon curry powder
- 8 cups (1.76 kg) sugar
- 2 litres vinegar

Cut up the vegetables but do not peel the cucumbers. Soak for 24 hours in a brine made from the salt and enough water to cover.

Next day heat it all up but don't boil, then strain it.

Mix all the dry ingredients, except the sugar, to a paste with a little vinegar.

Heat the rest of the vinegar and the sugar, then stir in the paste and continue to stir until it thickens. Add the vegetables and boil for 15 minutes only.

Bottle while hot.

Zucchini Muffins

MAKES 12

- 2 heaped cups (320 g) self-raising flour
- 1 tablespoon sugar
- pinch salt and ground white pepper
- pinch of curry powder
- 1 egg
- ½ cup (125 ml) grapeseed oil
- 1 cup (250 ml) milk
- 150 g (1 medium) zucchini (courgette), grated
- ¾ cup (90 g) grated cheese

In a bowl, mix all the dry ingredients together.

In a separate bowl beat the egg, then mix with the remaining wet ingredients.

Gently mix wet ingredients into dry ingredients. Do not overmix or beat as muffins will be tough.

Place large spoonfuls into a well-greased muffin tin. Bake in a 180°C oven for 25 minutes until golden.

Optional flavour extras:

- Add 125 g chopped bacon and ½ finely diced onion.
- OR 125 g chopped ham, ¾ cup (90 g) grated cheese and finely chopped chives.
- OR 1 small drained can sweet corn and ½ roasted capsicum (pepper), chopped.

Add the optional extras to the dry ingredients before mixing in the wet ingredients.

Pickled Zucchini

MAKES APPROXIMATELY 8 X 375 G JARS

- **2 kg zucchini (courgettes)**
- **6 large onions**
- **2 red capsicums (peppers)**
- **40 g salt**
- **iced water**
- **4 cups (880 g) raw sugar**
- **6 cups (1.5 litres) white vinegar**
- **2 teaspoons turmeric**
- **2 tablespoons mustard seeds**
- **2 teaspoons dill seeds**

Slice the zucchini and chop the other vegetables. Place in a bowl and sprinkle with salt, cover with iced water and leave for 3 hours.

Put the remaining ingredients into a large pan and bring to the boil.

Drain the vegetables and add them to the pan, boil for 1 minute.

Bottle in sterilised jars.

TIP

Zucchini (courgettes) can be grated and placed into ziplock bags and frozen. When ready to use, drain over a colander to remove the excess water. Use in bolognese sauce, casseroles or soups to add extra vegetables.

Zucchini Pickles

MAKES APPROXIMATELY 6 X 375 G JARS

- 3 cups (750 ml) white vinegar
- 750 g white sugar
- 1½ teaspoons caraway seeds
- 2 teaspoons turmeric
- 3 teaspoons dry mustard
- ¼ cup (35 g) salt
- 1 red capsicum (pepper), deseeded and chopped
- 1.5 kg zucchini (courgettes), grated and left to drain out any liquid in a colander
- 3 brown onions, peeled and finely chopped
- 2–3 cobs corn, kernels cut from the cob
- 5 cloves garlic, peeled and finely chopped
- 2 red chillies, finely chopped (remove seeds if you prefer your pickles not hot)
- 2 tablespoons cornflour and extra vinegar to mix to a paste

Boil together the vinegar, sugar, spices, salt and capsicum, then add drained zucchini, onion, corn, garlic and chillies. Cook for approximately 20 minutes, then thicken with the cornflour and extra vinegar. Bottle in clean, sterilised jars and seal.

Zucchini Fritters

Grate 2 medium zucchini (courgettes), add 1 peeled and very finely diced brown onion, 1 peeled and finely chopped clove garlic and salt and pepper to taste, 1 egg and about 2 tablespoons plain flour. Mix together well, then fry spoonfuls in a small amount of oil until golden brown. Corn, capsicum (pepper), tomato, chilli, grated haloumi cheese and your favourite spices can be added to change the flavours. A little curry powder lifts the flavour too.

Zucchini Dill Pickles

MAKES 1 LITRE

- 2 zucchini (courgettes), trimmed and thinly sliced
- 2 tablespoons fresh dill
- 1 teaspoon coriander seeds
- 1 teaspoon yellow mustard seeds
- ½ teaspoon black peppercorns
- 1 cup (250 ml) white vinegar
- 1 tablespoon salt
- 1 tablespoon sugar

Arrange the zucchini, dill, coriander seeds, mustard seeds and peppercorns in a 4 cup (1 litre) sterilised jar.

Place vinegar, salt, sugar and 1 cup (250 ml) water in a saucepan over medium heat. Bring to a simmer.

Carefully pour the vinegar mixture over the zucchini mixture. Seal tightly with a lid. Let stand for 2 weeks before using to develop the flavours.

Zucchini Soup

SERVES 6–8

- approximately 500 g zucchini (courgettes), sliced
- 2 brown onions, peeled and finely chopped
- 2 cloves garlic, peeled and finely chopped
- 1 large potato, peeled and finely diced
- oil, for frying
- 2 litres chicken stock
- 100–150 g blue cheese
- 125 ml pouring cream

Sauté the vegetables in a little oil until softened. Add the chicken stock and bring to the boil. Reduce the heat and simmer for approximately 30 minutes. Blend with a stick blender until smooth. Add the blue cheese and allow to melt, and add the pouring cream just before serving.

Variations: If desired a little fresh finely chopped basil OR thyme OR coriander can be added to serve for extra, or a change of, flavour. Also, this soup can be made using broccoli instead of zucchini.

Creamy Zucchini Soup

SERVES 6–8

- 1 tablespoon butter
- 2 medium brown onions, peeled and chopped or 1 leek, chopped
- 2 spring onions, chopped
- 1 clove garlic, peeled and crushed
- 1½ teaspoons dried basil
- 2 potatoes, peeled and diced
- 8–10 medium zucchini (courgettes)
- 2 litres vegetable stock
- salt and pepper, to taste
- 2 tablespoons chopped parsley
- ½ can (190 ml) evaporated milk or pouring cream

Melt butter in a large saucepan, add both types of onion and stir until onions are soft and translucent. Add garlic and basil after onion has been cooking for a few minutes so they don't burn. Add potato and roughly chopped zucchini. Stir until all is covered with the butter mixture.

Cover the vegetables with stock, add the pepper and cook till the potato and zucchini are soft. Blend soup and add salt to taste. Add parsley and evaporated milk or cream.

Zucchini Casserole

SERVES 4 AS A SIDE DISH

- 500 g zucchini (courgettes)
- 1 brown onion, peeled and chopped
- 60 g butter
- 60 g grated cheese
- ½ teaspoon salt and pepper
- 2 eggs, beaten
- ½ cup (50 g) breadcrumbs
- 1 tablespoon melted butter

Cut zucchini into slices. Fry onion in butter until soft.

Combine zucchini, onion, cheese, seasoning and eggs and mix well. Place in a greased ovenproof dish. Mix breadcrumbs with melted butter and sprinkle over the mixture. Bake at 160°C for 35–40 minutes.

Zucchini and Pineapple Jam

MAKES APPROXIMATELY 6 X 375 G JARS

- 1 fresh pineapple, peeled, cored and chopped finely
- Weigh the fresh pineapple flesh and grate the same weight in zucchini (courgettes) – you need 3½ cups of pineapple and zucchini combined.
- 3½ cups (770 g) sugar
- juice of 2 lemons
- 25 g commercial pectin (Jamsetta), if needed

Put pineapple and zucchini into a pot. Cook, adding the sugar and lemon juice for pectin. If you find you have more than 3½ cups pineapple/zucchini, then adjust the sugar to match.

Cook jam, stirring occasionally, until a little gels on a saucer. If it won't set, add 25 g pectin for the last 5 minutes of cooking.

Pour into sterilised jars, seal and label.

Zucchini and Pea Fritters

SERVES 2

- 2 medium zucchini (courgettes), grated
- ½ cup (80 g) frozen peas
- ½ cup (60 g) grated tasty cheese
- ⅓ cup (50 g) plain flour
- 2 eggs, lightly beaten
- 1 teaspoon curry powder
- vegetable oil, to fry

In a bowl mix all ingredients together, except the oil, and season well with salt and pepper. Heat some oil in a large frying pan. Drop spoonfuls of mixture into hot oil and cook on medium heat on both sides until golden brown. Cook in batches. Drain on paper towel and serve hot.

- **Marmalade is technically a jam** and traditionally made with citrus fruits as the main flavour base ingredient and, as winter is citrus fruit season, that's a good time to make it.

Basic Marmalade Recipe

MAKES APPROXIMATELY 8 X 375 G JARS

- 1 kg citrus fruit (e.g. grapefruit, Seville oranges, lemons)
- 2 litres water
- 3 kg sugar

Finely slice or chop the fruit. Soak overnight in the water.

Next day boil the fruit and water for about 1 hour or until the peel is soft. Add sugar slowly, stirring to dissolve the sugar, then boil until setting point is reached when a small amount gels on a cold saucer – start testing after 30 minutes' boiling, but it could take up to 1 hour.

HINTS FOR MAKING MARMALADE

- **Peel MUST be soaked** to soften, then cooked before adding any sugar as once sugar is added, the peel stops cooking. Hard uncooked peel is awful and spoils your marmalade. It's best to use finely sliced not chopped peel, but as long as your peel is soaked and cooked well, it is a matter of personal choice.

- **Any citrus fruit or combination of fruit can be used.** Once you are happy with your base of citrus, don't be afraid to experiment with your flavours. Try adding ½ to 1 finely chopped and deseeded chilli to grapefruit marmalade, or mandarin and carrot. BUT your secondary flavours must not overpower the base citrus marmalade flavour.

- If making your marmalade from **limes**, the rind needs longer soaking than other varieties of citrus to soften.

- To test for **setting point** – a) put a couple of spoonfuls on a chilled saucer, place in the fridge for a few minutes, then if you can pull a knife through and leave a trail, setting point has been reached, OR, b) if you place a little of the marmalade on a chilled saucer, leave for about 30 seconds, then when you run your finger over it, it 'wrinkles', setting point has been reached.

Steamed Orange Pudding

You will need 2 eggs – plus their weight in softened butter, caster sugar and self-raising flour, and the juice and rind of 1 orange. Cream butter and sugar well, add eggs one at a time, beat well. Then add the sifted self-raising flour and lastly the rind and juice of 1 orange. Place in a greased pudding basin and steam for 1 hour to 1½ hours. Serve with warmed marmalade and custard OR place some marmalade in the bottom of the steamer basin before pouring in the pudding mixture to make a steamed upside down marmalade pudding.

• Lamb Ribs with a Marmalade Glaze

Mix together ¼ cup (80 g) marmalade, 2 tablespoons soy sauce, 2 cloves crushed garlic, and 2 tablespoons sweet chilli sauce. Marinate lamb ribs in the marinade for 3 hours in the refrigerator. Place the ribs in a baking dish and bake in a moderate (180°C) oven for 1 hour, basting with the marinade frequently.

TIPS

• If you have a little **left-over marmalade** in the bottom of the jar, add it to a casserole to give a flavour zing.

• Add 1 tablespoon to a **fruit cake** or sultana cake mixture for extra flavour.

• Mix marmalade with a little soy sauce and brush over a **Christmas leg of ham** before baking.

TIPS FOR SAVOURY PRESERVES

As with all types of preserving, the produce you are going to use in your more savoury preserves should be in **good condition** and not overripe.

Remember also the necessity of **safety in your kitchen** – the produce is often at boiling point, so children and pets should not be close to your work space. Make sure loose mats or objects likely to trip you up are removed before you start.

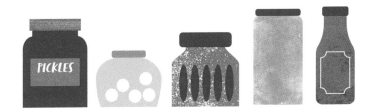

TIPS FOR SAUCES

- Sauces **made from fruit and/or vegetables** are flavoured and cooked in vinegar. The whole is strained or sieved to give a smooth pouring product. This is re-cooked and bottled.

- Some sauces with a higher proportion of **vinegar** are thin, the classic example being Worcestershire. Fruit and vegetable sauces are thicker, personal preference dictating how thick the finished sauce is.

- As with other pickled goods, vinegar is the **preservative** and it must be in a high enough proportion to achieve this purpose.

- Sauces are subject to **separating** out. This is usually due to insufficient cooking when the vinegar is added. Overripe fruit will also cause separation.

- Many fruits and vegetables can be used, alone or in combination. Fruit should be **ripe but not overripe** for sauce making.

- Sauce should be mild, sweet, tart, hot or fiery. The spices used to **flavour** sauces are best used whole and tied in a muslin bag if bright, well coloured products are wanted.

- **Bottling** of sauces must be done immediately. Use a funnel to make this easier.

- After the bottle is **sealed**, invert so that the air gap is heated by the hot sauce. This will help to preserve the product.

Spicy Plum Sauce

Very good as a dipping sauce for spring rolls.

- **4 Granny Smith apples**
- **2–3 red chillies, seeded and finely cut**
- **2 kg dark plums (Satsuma or blood), chopped**
- **4 cups (880 g) brown sugar**
- **2 cups (500 ml) malt vinegar**
- **2 large onions, finely chopped**
- **⅔ cup (170 ml) soy sauce**
- **4 tablespoons grated fresh ginger**
- **4 large cloves garlic, finely chopped**
- **2 teaspoons allspice**
- **1½ teaspoons cloves**

Peel, core and finely chop the apples, then cook with 2 cups (500 ml) of water until soft.

Add all ingredients to the apple mix and cook gently for approximately 40 minutes, stirring to prevent the sauce burning or catching.

Once cooked, press though a coarse strainer or colander to remove skins and stones and larger particles.

Place in a clean pan and cook further until slightly thickened.

Pour sauce into cleaned and sterilised jars with screw lids, which have also been sterilised, then seal.

Sauce is best left to mature for 3–4 weeks before use. Once opened use within 4–6 weeks and store in the refrigerator.

Worcestershire Sauce

MAKES APPROXIMATELY 6 X 375 G JARS

- **1.2 litres vinegar, plus a little extra if needed**
- **1 cup (350 g) treacle**
- **7 g pepper**
- **7 g mace**
- **7 g cayenne pepper**
- **7 g garlic**
- **7 g cloves**
- **340 g brown onions, sliced**
- **cornflour, if needed**

Soak all, except the cornflour, for 14 days, then bring to the boil and simmer for ½ hour, strain then bring to the boil again.

If you like it a little thicker, make a paste of a little cornflour mixed with a little cold vinegar and reboil.

Bottle into hot sterilised jars.

Pickled Onions

MAKES 2 LARGE WIDE-MOUTHED JARS

- 1.5 kg pickling onions
- ½ cup (150 g) salt
- water

FOR EACH JAR ALLOW:
- 2 black peppercorns
- 1 small chilli
- 1 whole clove
- white or malt vinegar

Peel onions and put in a large non-metallic bowl, sprinkle with salt and add enough cold water to cover. Cover and allow to stand for 24 hours.

Drain onions, rinse in cold water, then place in sterilised jars. Turn upside down on thick newspaper, covered with paper towel, and drain a further 24 hours.

Turn up the right way and add to each jar peppercorns, chilli and the clove. Fill with white or malt vinegar to cover onions. Seal with cork or plastic lid. Store about 4 weeks before use.

WHAT WENT
WRONG?

HELPFUL KITCHEN TIPS

- To correct **over salting** a dish, try adding a little brown sugar.

- Never store **potatoes and onions** in the same container. The onions make the potatoes go soft. Always store potatoes and onions in a dark airy cupboard to stop potatoes going green. Light also makes potatoes and onions shoot. Never eat the potatoes if they have gone green.

- When **measuring honey or syrup**, grease the measuring cup with cooking oil and rinse in hot water before using. This assists in a more accurate measure and prevents being left with a sticky cup.

- When a recipe calls for **½ cup chopped nuts** (or other ingredient) it means chop the nuts, then measure; whereas **½ cup nuts (or other ingredient), chopped**, means measure the nuts, then chop them.

- **Shrinking and drying** out is usually a result of poor covering of the product, allowing moisture to evaporate, or warm storage conditions. To fix, remove dry part and use the remainder.

- **Syrupy** liquid on top of dish? Moisture not sufficiently evaporated in cooking, needs longer cooking with the lid off. Use before too long as storage time will be limited.

TIPS FOR TENDER MEAT

- Always bring meat to **room temperature** before cooking to help keep it tender.

- **Don't preheat oven** before placing meat in to cook. Turn the oven on as you place the meat into it. Placing the meat into a cold oven will help to tenderise it. The only exception is roast pork when you put the pork into a hot oven to start to get the crackling.

- Adding a small sprinkle of bicarbonate of soda to cheaper cuts of meat such as chuck steak, helps to **tenderise** it.

- Juice of 1 lemon added to water can help to **tenderise cheaper cuts of meat**.

- Add ¼ cup (60 ml) apple cider vinegar to a pot of water to cook **corned beef** to help to tenderise it. For extra flavouring, add 1 peeled but whole onion, 12 whole cloves and 20 whole black peppercorns.

TROUBLESHOOTING TIPS FOR PRESERVES, MARMALADES AND JELLIES

- **Rind of marmalade is hard**

  Always soak finely sliced marmalade fruit in water overnight, then cook for 1 hour before adding sugar. Make sure rind is soft before adding sugar because once sugar is added, the rind will not soften any further, no matter how long you cook the marmalade.

- **Marmalade fruit floats to the top**

  Marmalade needs to sit for a few minutes before bottling, so do not pour into the jars when marmalade has just come off the boil. Never put any hot preserve into hot jars or the preserve will boil over out of the jar.

- **Marmalade is cloudy**

  Too much pith of the citrus fruit has been left on the sliced fruit.

- **Jelly is cloudy**

  When pouring cooked fruit such as quinces or crabapples into the jelly bag to drain, never squeeze the jelly bag as this causes cloudiness in your finished jelly product.

- **Jelly won't set**

  Usually occurs when the fruit used to make the jelly was too ripe and too low in pectin, or because the jelly was not boiled long enough to reach the setting point. Reboil and use commercial pectin (Jamsetta) according to packet instructions.

- **Too spicy**

  Boil up a quantity of the basic fruit and vegetable in vinegar, but without any flavouring. When this is soft add INTO IT some of the over-spiced product. Check the taste and keep mixing the two until satisfied. The whole of the new mixture must be boiled before bottling. Can also be used when a product is too salty.

- **Mould**
Imperfectly cleaned jars and lids, or warm damp storage area.

- **Syrupy jelly**
The jelly was overcooked or there was not enough pectin in the fruit to begin with. If you used fruit with low pectin level, reboil the jelly with some lemon juice or commercial pectin (Jamsetta). Remember to wash and resterilise the jars you've used.

- **Jam too dark**
Poor quality fruit has been used in the making of the jam or it has been cooked too long so that the sugar has caramelised.

- **Scum on jam**
Put a knob of butter in the jam pan as you are cooking the jam. It stops the scum and the scum does not reappear.

- **There's a vinegar collar when making sauce, pickles or chutney**
Preserve has not boiled long enough to evaporate some of the liquid. Reboil to evaporate some of the liquid and bottle in resterilised jars.

- **If your fruit overripens** before you have time to make jam, add juice of a lemon for every kilogram of fruit or a little commercial pectin (Jamsetta) according to packet instructions.

- **If using frozen fruit** to make jam (e.g. plums or apricots), fully thaw it out and tip off a little of the liquid before you start to cook up the jam.

- **Puff pastry problems**

Uneven lift can happen for a number of reasons. It can be caused by uneven rolling out of the pastry, uneven distribution of fat prior to rolling out or because the oven heats unevenly. Poor lift can also be caused by overworking the pastry, rolling it out too thinly, incorrect proportion of fat – either too much or too little – or because the pastry wasn't rested and chilled before rolling.

- **If your pastry shrinks**

Pastry was not rested or chilled enough to allow the gluten in the flour to relax.

- **If fat runs out of the pastry when cooking**

Your oven temperature was not set high enough, too much fat as a proportion was used and the pastry was under-rolled, making the layers too thick.

- **Rustic fruit tart without a soggy bottom**

If making a 'rustic' tart, roll out shortcrust pastry and sprinkle with rice flour or ground rice. Place halved apricots or plums over this (or tomatoes for a savoury tart) and fold in the edges of the tart. The rice flour will absorb some of the juice from the fruit as it cooks so you don't get a soggy bottom on the tart. Brush the fruit with a little melted jam of the same flavour as the fruit and bake in a moderate (180°C) oven for approximately 25 minutes.

- **Sugar spots on the top of the cooked cake**

Butter and sugar were not creamed well enough together. If you roll a little of the creamed butter and sugar between thumb and finger, there should not be a gritty feel if the butter and sugar have been creamed well. If there is a gritty feeling, then continue to beat longer. Using caster sugar in cakes gives a finer texture.

- **Muffins tough with large holes**

Mix dry ingredients and separately mix the liquid ingredients before mixing together gently. Don't beat muffin mixture or this will also make them tough. It doesn't matter if there is a little of the mixture not properly mixed in before baking.

- **Cake does not rise**

Oven is too cool. Always preheat your oven before placing a cake in it. If it is too cool, the chemical action that makes a cake rise may fail to take place. Using stale flour could also contribute to poor rising.

- **Cake has a coarse dry texture**

Not enough liquid in the cake mixture.

- **To test if a cake is baked well** use a fine cake tester. If it comes out clean from being inserted gently into the centre of the cake, it is cooked. Alternatively, if the cake is shrinking away from the side of the tin or if the cake springs back when you touch it lightly with your finger, your cake is ready to take out of the oven.

• Cake sinks in the centre
Too much sugar or liquid or too hot an oven, or too coarse a sugar (use caster sugar), or cake is undercooked.

• Excessive shrinking of cake
Wrong balance of ingredients, or too much sugar or liquid, or the oven temperature was too high, or the cake was overcooked.

• Cracked top in the cake
The tin used was not large enough, or the oven temperature was too high.

• Hole in the cake when cut
Mixture was not creamed sufficiently, or oven set at too high a temperature, or too much raising agent was used.

• Cake crusty, overbrowned, but uncooked in the centre
Not enough sugar or liquid, or the cake cooked at too high a temperature, or cake tin used was too small causing the top to overcook with the centre undercooked.

• Rock buns or other small 'drop' cakes run
The mixture was too soft or the oven was too cool when they went in.

• **Sticky meringues** are caused by undercooking or trying to cook them too quickly. Cool meringues in the oven, then store in an airtight container as exposure to the air will make meringues sticky.

• Swiss roll cracks
Oven was too cool when cooking, allowing the mixture to form a crust which then cracks when you try to roll it up with the filling.

· **Burnt edges on fruit cakes**
Cake cooked in too hot an oven or left in the oven too long and overcooked. Fruit cakes should always be cooked in a very cool oven – 100–120°C.

· **Sinking fruit in fruit cake**
Fruit cake mixture was too moist and slack.

· **Streaks in the cooked cake**
Batter not mixed adequately before placing in the tin to bake.

· **Pavlova/meringue**
Always have the eggs at room temperature, never straight from the fridge. Make sure the bowl you are beating egg whites in is very clean and dry. Any sign of grease and the egg whites won't whip up. Vinegar in a pavlova recipe is the ingredient that makes the marshmallow centre.

TROUBLESHOOTING TIPS FOR BISCUITS

- **Biscuits spread too much while baking**
  This could be because they were placed on warm trays (they should
  be cool before using), the mixture could have been overbeaten, or the
  ingredients may have been incorrectly measured (too much liquid
  or insufficient flour), or the wrong type of flour was used, or the oven
  was not hot enough to set the mixture quickly.

- **Biscuits too soft**
  The ingredients may have been incorrectly measured, or baked at
  too low a temperature or for not long enough. Once cool, place them
  back in the oven for a few more minutes. (If stacked on top of each
  other on trays for cooling, they can also become soft. Also, don't place
  them in storage containers before the biscuits are cold.)

- **Biscuits too pale**
  It could be due to insufficient cooking time or oven temperature
  being too low.

- **Biscuits too dark**
  This may be due to overcooking or too high an oven temperature.

- **Biscuits too hard**
  The ingredients may have been incorrectly measured, or baked at too
  high a temperature or for too long.

- **Biscuits too brown underneath**
  The trays may be incorrectly positioned in the oven (tray too large or
  preventing air circulation or placed too low in the oven). Trays were
  over-greased, or too high a temperature can cause over-browning as
  can over-measuring sweet ingredients.

INDEX

Published in 2022 by Murdoch Books, an imprint of Allen & Unwin

Murdoch Books Australia
83 Alexander Street
Crows Nest NSW 2065
Phone: +61 (0)2 8425 0100
murdochbooks.com.au
info@murdochbooks.com.au

Murdoch Books UK
Ormond House
26–27 Boswell Street
London WC1N 3JZ
Phone: +44 (0) 20 8785 5995
murdochbooks.co.uk
info@murdochbooks.co.uk

For corporate orders and custom publishing, contact our business development team at
salesenquiries@murdochbooks.com.au

Publisher: Corinne Roberts
Editorial Manager: Justin Wolfers
Design Manager: Kristy Allen
Designer and Illustrator: Julia Cornelius
Editor: Ariana Klepac
Production Director: Lou Playfair

*We acknowledge that we meet and work on the traditional lands of the Cammeraygal people of the Eora Nation
and pay our respects to their elders past, present and future.*

ISBN 9 781 92235 199 9 Australia

A catalogue record for this
book is available from the
National Library of Australia
NATIONAL
LIBRARY
OF AUSTRALIA

A catalogue record for this book is available from the British Library

Printed by McPherson's Printing Group

OVEN GUIDE: You may find cooking times vary depending on the oven you are using. For fan-forced ovens,
as a general rule, set the oven temperature to 20°C (70°F) lower than indicated in the recipe.
TABLESPOON MEASURES: We have used 20 ml (4 teaspoon) tablespoon measures. If you are using a 15 ml
(3 teaspoon) tablespoon add an extra teaspoon of the ingredient for each tablespoon specified.

10 9 8 7 6 5 4 3 2 1